English World

Student's Book

7 A2+

Mary Bowen, Liz Hocking & Wendy Wren

Unit	Reading	Reading comprehension	Working with words	Grammar
1 Magazines Page 7	*The portrait project* a magazine article including an interview	literal questions; gapfill; thinking skills; scanning; personal response	word classes; suffix *-tion*; spelling: *ss* sounding *sh*	present tenses: present simple *They work for a magazine.* present continuous *Today they are reporting on a new project.*
2 City life Page 17	*The man at the fountain* a descriptive narrative	multiple choice; thinking skills; adjective recognition; scanning; personal response	present participle adjectives; prefixes and suffixes; spelling: doubling final consonant before suffixing	past tenses: past simple + past continuous *While Philippe was watching him, the man pointed his camera.* *while* and *when*
3 Life at the edge Page 27	*Endangered animals in the north* an information text	literal questions; meanings of headings; thinking skills; definitions; personal response	adjectives with suffixes *-al* and *-y*; spelling: words with *ie / ei*	future: *will* predictions *In three days' time they will set out.* future: *going to* plans / intentions *They are going to count the otters.*
4 Advertisements Page 37	*Adventure sports centre* an advertisement	literal questions; adjective definitions; word choice; word classes; thinking skills; personal response	words ending *-ent / -ence* and *-ant / -ance*; spelling: words with *ou / oo*	present perfect *He has recently broken his arm.* *She hasn't tried the vertical slide.*
5 Great lives Page 47	*Victoria, Queen of the United Kingdom* a biography	true/false questions; definitions; thinking skills; scanning; personal response	suffixes: *-ment / -ness* spelling: words with *gu*	comparative adjectives: *as ... as, not as ... as, -er than* *Victoria was not as free as other children.*
6 What a character! Page 57	*Mr Duffy's workshop* a description of a character	literal questions; noun phrases; thinking skills; words in context; personal response	words ending *-ate*; word classes; spelling: words with silent *c*	articles: *a, an, the,* zero article *Flowers filled the courtyard. An old peach tree was in the corner. Near the tree was a door.*
7 This is what to do Page 67	*Ben and Bella's Brilliantly Healthy Beefburgers* a recipe with instructions	literal questions; discussion of writing style; matching/ordering sentences; personal response	past participle adjectives; prefix *pre-*; spelling: words ending *-ture*	zero conditional *If you heat water to 100° Celsius, it boils.*
8 A point of view Page 77	*Wildlife World* a blog	true/false questions; style discussion; definitions; scanning; thinking skills; personal response	negative prefixes: *in- / im-*; homophones; spelling: words with *ci / ti*	first conditional with *if / unless* *You will see different animals if you visit the zoo.* *Unless people are given information, they will go on visiting zoos.*
9 How the body works Page 87	*How we see* an explanatory text	literal questions; multiple choice; thinking skills; vocabulary; personal response	suffixes: *-ible / -able*; gerunds; spelling: words ending *-sion*	the passive: present, past, present perfect, future *The eye is protected by the eyelid.* *The eye was / will be / has been damaged.*
10 Later that day ... Page 97	*A helping hand* a narrative story	true/false questions; thinking skills; vocabulary; synonyms and antonyms; personal response	extra information in clauses; suffix *-ous*; spelling: words ending *-er / -re*	present perfect simple and continuous *for / since* *She has been interested in photography for a long time.* *She has been taking photos since her seventh birthday.*
11 Sports reports Page 107	*A match with a difference* a newspaper sports report	multiple choice; thinking skills; definitions; matching paragraphs to summaries; personal response	compound nouns; hyphenated words; spelling: words with *-tch*	reported speech *Someone shouted that the balloon was landing on the pitch.*
12 On stage Page 117	*Danger on the railway* a playscript based on a classic text	literal questions; thinking skills; synonyms; Who said it?; personal response	adverbial phrases; suffix *-ive*; spelling: words with modified *a* after *w*	second conditional *If a train came along the line now, it would crash.*

Grammar extra pages 127–130   Project pages 131–135

Grammar in use	Writing Individual writing (WB)	Listening and speaking
stative verbs *I live in … / I go to … school. /* *I like / I've got …*	features of interviews SB: an interview with Holly WB: an interview with Ross	**Conversation practice:** introducing yourself **Listening comprehension:** a description of family members and the jobs they do **Individual speaking (WB):** talking about your family
used to *I used to go to school.*	features of descriptive writing SB: a square at night WB: a square in the rain	**Conversation practice:** first person memories: *I used to …* **Listening comprehension:** a recount of childhood from a grandma **Individual speaking (WB):** a family member's childhood
present continuous for future events *I'm meeting my cousin in the morning.*	study skills note taking and drafting SB: a paragraph about the sea otter WB: a report about the giant panda	**Conversation practice:** plans for the week **Listening comprehension:** a description of a planned trip to London **Individual speaking (WB):** personal future plans
present perfect with *for, since, just* and *yet* *They've just scored.* *Have they won the match yet?* *Joe has been in the team for six weeks / since May.*	features of persuasive writing SB: handout for a basketball final WB: handout for a school competition	**Conversation practice:** a dialogue about tasks done / not done yet **Listening comprehension:** an interview with a basketball team captain **Individual speaking (WB):** talking about what you have done / haven't done this week
superlative adjectives; irregular comparative / superlative adjectives *good, better, best; bad, worse, worst*	features of biographies SB: a biography of Elizabeth I WB: a biography of a relative	**Conversation practice:** a personal dialogue about favourite things to do: *the most interesting, the best*, etc. **Listening comprehension:** an extract from a TV programme **Individual speaking (WB):** your best project
verb + *-ing* *I enjoy working.* verb + infinitive *I want to study.*	features of portraying character SB: a description of Mrs Duffy WB: a description of George	**Conversation practice:** a dialogue about future career plans: *I don't like working indoors. I want to be a mountain guide.* **Listening comprehension:** a monologue about future career plans **Individual speaking (WB):** future career plans
quantifiers with countable / uncountable nouns: *some, any, a lot of, lots of, much, many, a few, a little*	features of writing instructions SB: instructions for making fish burgers WB: instructions for making scrambled eggs	**Conversation practice:** a dialogue about things in local shops / shopping centre **Listening comprehension:** conversations from different shops **Individual speaking (WB):** talking about a favourite shop
modal verbs: *may, might, can, could, should, ought to, must* *We ought not to build on the open spaces.* *This park may be lost forever.*	features of expressing a point of view SB: an opinion of mobile phones WB: an opinion of homework	**Conversation practice:** talking about buildings **Listening comprehension:** a council's plans for new buildings **Individual speaking (WB):** talking about new buildings in your town or city
question tags *It's busy, isn't it?* *She doesn't look busy, does she?*	features of explanations SB: an explanation of how the lungs work WB: an explanation of getting ready and travelling to school	**Conversation practice:** a dialogue about a market **Listening comprehension:** an interview with a market stall holder **Individual speaking (WB):** talking about a local market or one visited elsewhere
present perfect with *ever / never* contrasted with past tense *Have you ever tried Morris dancing?* *I've never seen it.*	features of story plots SB: writing the next part of the narrative story WB: planning and writing a story with a simple plot	**Conversation practice:** a dialogue about festivals and celebrations around the world **Listening comprehension:** a conversation at a festival **Individual speaking (WB):** talking about a festival
defining relative clauses with *which, who, that, where, when* *There are some streets where cars are banned.*	features of newspapers and magazines SB: a newspaper sports report WB: a newspaper report about a person	**Conversation practice:** a dialogue about methods of transport **Listening comprehension:** train information announcements **Individual speaking (WB):** recounting a journey
modals: *have to, had to, don't have to, must, mustn't* *I had to edit the video.* *We must finish the project.* *We mustn't send it off late.*	features of playscripts SB: writing the play scene from a different viewpoint WB: writing the next scene of the play	**Conversation practice:** a dialogue about tasks to be done **Listening comprehension:** an email **Individual speaking (WB):** talking about past, present and future tasks

Introducing ...

Laura Hardy

age	15
lives in	West Hill, Hampton
brother	Jack, aged 12
school	West Hill Academy
interests/hobbies	computer technology, photography, films (with special effects)
likes	cartoon films, the internet (I love it!!)
dislikes	going to the dentist

Jack Hardy

age	12
lives in	West Hill, Hampton
sister	Laura, aged 15
school	West Hill Academy
interests/hobbies	swimming, music
likes	beach holidays, talking to people, Chinese food
dislikes	long car journeys, too much homework

Holly Carter

age	14
lives in	Hampton town centre
brother	Micky, aged 9
sisters	Nancy, aged 9; Tammy, aged 6
school	Central High School
interests/hobbies	design (especially clothes), doing puzzles and quizzes
likes	fashion, shopping
dislikes	cold weather (especially wet, cold weather), too much homework

Ross Lawrence

age	14
lives in	North Park, Hampton
brother	Harry, aged 16
sister	Amy, aged 10
school	North Park College
interests/hobbies	art, swimming, basketball
likes	animals (all of them but particularly my cat, Claws)
dislikes	zoos, people who are cruel to animals

The Language Lab

Magazines

Check-in
You can buy magazines about all kinds of different topics: sport, fashion, music, films and film stars, news and TV.

List the names of magazines that you know.
How often do you read a magazine? Which one?
Do you like it? Why? / Why not?
If you could read another magazine, what would it be?

You are going to read pages from a magazine for young people.

Reading
- A **magazine article** about the start of the *Portrait* project for school students. The article is set out in **columns**.
- The article includes an **interview**. The interview is set out like a **play**.

How is a play set out?

- These words are in the article.

    technology   volunteer   create   session
    construct   imagination

What do they mean? Check in your dictionary.

Vocabulary and spelling
- Learn words to do with working on a **group project**.
- Learn about words ending **-tion**.
- Learn about spelling **words with ss sounding sh**.

Have you ever done a project in a group?
What was it? Who did you work with?

Grammar
- Practise **present tenses**: present simple, present continuous.
- Practise verbs usually used in the **simple form**.
- Practise when to use **make** or **do**.

Writing
- Learn about the writing **features of an interview**.
- Compose **interview questions**.
- **Write an interview** using the questions.
- **Work out questions** and write an interview.

Listening
- Laura, Jack, Holly and Ross's discussion about planning their project.
- A **dialogue** in which Jack finds out about Ross.
- Ross **telling his new friends** about his family.

Have you met any new friends at school?

Speaking
- Talk to your friends; find out about them.
- Tell the class about **your family**.

How many people are there in your family at home?

Reading

Do you like... Art?  Technology?

Will Jones and *Patsy Parker* report on how these subjects meet in ...

The *portrait* project

Professor John Brown is running the project.

City Hall was buzzing with excitement last week. More than fifty enthusiastic volunteers came for the start of a new arts and technology project for school students.

In the project, *A portrait of our town*, students create a portrait of the place where they live. Professor Brown of Hampton University explained to them, "You must decide what to tell people about your town. You could tell them about buildings and places or you could tell them about some of the people who live there. It's your chance, too, to give your own opinions. What is happening in your town now? How do you feel about it?"

The students were evidently motivated by the professor's questions. After the first session, there was a rush for the leaflets about the project. Groups of boys and girls began to discuss ideas.

In the second session, Professor Brown talked about producing the portrait. "You can decide what to use," he explained, "film, photography, recordings of voices, sounds and music, different kinds of writing and art. The only limit on what you can do is your own imagination."

The students are aged from 12–16 and they come from different schools in all parts of the town. They are going to work in groups of 4–6. Most students met for the first time at City Hall. They had to choose who they would like to work with.

To help students to find out about each other, Professor Brown put up some message boards. One said *I like ...* Others said *I don't like ... I am interested in ...* Students were invited to respond by writing on pieces of paper and sticking them on the board.

While they were busy writing and reading responses, Professor Brown explained that students from all over the country are creating *Portraits*. Some of them live in very big cities. "But they don't have to include the whole city," he said. "They can construct a portrait of their part of it. It could be just their local neighbourhood."

A PORTRAIT OF OUR TOWN
National student project
How to begin
Ask yourself these questions ...

Reading: a magazine article and interview

We chatted to students at the message boards – a popular meeting place.

"This is great. I'm making new friends here today and I'm really enjoying it. I like making new friends!"
Holly Carter, 14

"Reading the messages is fun. I'm interested in people and I like finding out about them."
Ross Lawrence, 14

Fifteen-year-old Laura Hardy is the first student who volunteered to take part in the project. She's the subject of this week's …

Patsy Parker interview

Patsy: Why did you want to do this project, Laura?
Laura: I thought it sounded interesting. We're going to meet every week to work on the project. At the end of the year, we are going to present our finished portraits. I like creating things and I like looking at things and taking pictures of them.
Patsy: Are you interested in photography?
Laura: Yes, I am. I'm interested in film, too, and computers. I'm doing a computer animation project at school at the moment. I go to a computer club every Monday.
Patsy: Which school do you go to?
Laura: I go to West Hill Academy.
Patsy: Have you got any brothers or sisters?
Laura: Yes, I've got one brother, Jack. We go to the same school and he's here today, too … somewhere, but I can't see him. He's probably looking at the message board or he's chatting to someone. He likes talking to people.
Patsy: What things do you like?
Laura: Cartoon films and surfing the internet.
Patsy: Do you have any dislikes?
Laura: Not really … but I don't like going to the dentist much.
Patsy: Me neither!

Good luck to all the students working on the project. We'll tell you how they get on later in the year.

Reading comprehension

1 **Answer these questions.**
1. Which subjects come together in the new project?
2. Who are the writers of the magazine report?
3. Where did the group of volunteers meet?
4. Who is running the project?
5. What did Professor Brown tell the students they could use to create their portraits?
6. What age are the students who are doing this project?
7. How were students invited to respond to the message boards?
8. What could students who live in big cities do?
9. What did Ross say he was interested in?
10. How often does Laura go to a computer club?

2 **Choose the correct word or phrase to complete each sentence.**

> portrait   technology   volunteer   sessions   present   include   get on

1. I'm a bit nervous because I'm going to _____ my project to the class today.
2. Ben was fed up because he didn't _____ well in the computer lesson.
3. My brother is studying _____ at the university.
4. A huge _____ of Grandfather is hanging in the hall.
5. The lesson was very long so the teacher divided it into two _____.
6. Our teacher said that we didn't _____ enough pictures in our project.
7. "Is there a _____ who can help me carry these books?" asked the teacher.

3 **Think about the answers to these questions. Discuss your ideas.**
1. Why do you think there was a rush to get leaflets about the project after the first session?
2. Why was Holly enjoying the sessions at City Hall?
3. Why do you think the interview with Laura is included in the report?
4. What two things does Laura think Jack is probably doing? What kind of person do you think Jack is?
5. Do you think Laura and Jack get on well together? How do you know?

4 **Scan the text and find:**
1. three words for places where people learn
   _____   _____   _____
2. two words that mean *talk*
   _____   _____
3. three words that mean the same, or nearly the same, as *make*
   _____   _____   _____

Your views
- Do you like working in a group? Why? / Why not?
- What is the best project you have ever done?
- Did you do it on your own or with others?
- Why was it your best project?

---

10 Reading comprehension: literal, inferential and deductive questions; vocabulary: synonyms; personal response

Working with words

A Word classes

1 Read these words from the article, by Will Jones and Patsy Parker, then read all the questions. Write the answers.

> present   session   get on   technology
> volunteer   include   portrait

If you aren't sure, check in your dictionary!

1 Which words are used as nouns?
_____ _____
_____ _____

2 Which words are used as verbs?
_____ _____
_____ _____

3 Which word is used as both a noun and a verb?
_____

4 Which word is used as a verb in the report but is a noun when it is pronounced differently?
_____

B Making new words

- A lot of words in English end with *-tion*. This ending sounds /ʃən/.
  sta**tion**   na**tion**

It's called the root word because it's the part that you start with.

1 The ending *-tion* can often be added to another word. This word is called the root word. Read these pairs of words and answer the questions.

root word	new word
invite	invitation
imagine	imagination
animate	animation
motivate	motivation
create	creation
produce	production
construct	construction
present	presentation

The endings of some verbs ending -e change when -tion is added.

1 What class of word is the root word?
2 What class of word is made by adding *-tion*?

2 Read the words in Activity 1 again. Which *-tion* words were in the report by Will Jones and Patsy Parker?
_____ _____

An ending that can be added to a word to make a new word is called a suffix.

C Spelling
ss sounding sh

- In some words double s sounds like *sh*.
  e.g. se**ss**ion.
  There was a rush at the end of the se**ss**ion.

1 Read these words aloud then answer the questions.

> discussion   mission   impression   procession

1 Can you find a root word that means *to talk about*? _____

2 Look at the other words. Can you find a word inside one of them that means *to push down*?
_____

2 Match each word in Activity 1 to the correct definition. Use your dictionary to help you.

1 the mark left on something by pressing on it
_____

2 a talk between two or more people about something
_____

3 a number of people walking forwards together
_____

4 a task done by an individual or a group
_____

Working with words: word classes; words ending *-tion*; ss sounding *sh*

Grammar

1 Read.

Will Jones and Patsy Parker are reporters. They **work** for 'Teen Talk', a popular magazine for young people. They **report** on all sorts of things, such as sport, fashion, music, books and films. They often **meet** interesting people and **interview** them.

Today Will and Patsy are at City Hall, where they **are reporting** on a new project called *A portrait of our town*. They **are interviewing** Professor John Brown, who **is running** the project. Professor Brown **teaches** English at Hampton University but he **is not teaching** today. He **is explaining** the *Portrait* project to Will and Patsy.

2 Answer these questions.
1. What do Will and Patsy do?
2. What do they report on?
3. Who do they often meet?
4. Who are Will and Patsy interviewing today?
5. Why are they interviewing Professor Brown?
6. Where does Professor Brown work?
7. What does he teach?
8. What is Professor Brown talking about with Will and Patsy?

3 Ask and answer. Use the present simple.
1. Which magazine – Will and Patsy – work for?
   A: Which magazine do Will and Patsy work for?
   B: They work for 'Teen Talk'.
2. Who – they – often – interview?
3. What – they – write about?
4. Patsy – report on fashion?
5. Who – they – meet?
6. Where – Professor Brown – teach?
7. he – teach – Russian?
8. What – he – teach?

4 Look at the picture above. Correct the sentences.
1. Professor Brown is interviewing the reporters.
2. Professor Brown is recording the interview.
3. The young reporters are speaking.
4. Will Jones is making notes.
5. Professor Brown is wearing glasses.
6. Professor Brown and Will are wearing jackets.
7. Patsy is holding the microphone.
8. Will is looking at Patsy.

5 Write and talk. Answer the questions. Then discuss your answers.
1. What do you do every day?
2. What do you often do at the weekend?
3. What do you never do?
4. What are you doing now?
5. What are you wearing today?
6. How are you feeling today?

> **Remember!**
> - Use the present simple for things that happen regularly.
>   *Joe **watches** TV every day.*
> - Use the present continuous for things that are happening now.
>   *At the moment he **is watching** his favourite programme.*

- Think of some more sentences using the present simple and the present continuous.

Grammar in use

City Hall
A Portrait of our town
Session 2
Form a group!
Plan your project

1 Listen and read.

Ross: Well, where shall we start?
Holly: Shall we introduce ourselves?
Laura: Good idea. My name's Laura and this is my brother, Jack.
Ross: Hi. I'm Ross and this is Holly.
Laura: Hello! Nice to meet you.
Jack: I **think** this *Portrait* project is a great idea.
Laura: Me, too. It **sounds** brilliant.
Holly: What are we going to include? We should decide.
Ross: The river? Interesting buildings?
Jack: Famous people in the town? Our football team?
Laura: Let's make a list.
Holly: How can we all help?
Jack: Yes, what **do** we all **like** doing? I **mean**, what are we good at?
Laura: I **like** computers and photography. I**'ve got** a video camera.
Holly: Great! That's useful. We **need** equipment like that.
Ross: I'm good at art and I **love** sport.
Holly: Well, I **hate** sport. I **prefer** fashion and going shopping.
Laura: You could do something on the new shopping centre. It's the grand opening next week.
Holly: I **know**! I can't wait! All those new shops!
Jack: OK. Let's write down some ideas. Number 1: Shopping centre. What else?

2 Answer these questions.

1. Where are the teenagers and what are they doing?
2. What do Jack and Laura think of the project?
3. What do they need to make?
4. What does Laura like? What useful equipment has she got?
5. What does Ross love?
6. Who hates sport?

3 Complete the sentences with verbs from the box. Use the present simple.

> think   sound   like   mean
> need   prefer   know

1. The *Portrait* project _____ brilliant.
2. Professor Brown _____ many interesting facts about the town.
3. Laura _____ the project is brilliant.
4. The girls _____ tennis but the boys _____ swimming.
5. What _____ the word *imagination* _____?
6. The teenagers _____ to plan their project.

4 Talk about it.

1. What do you love and what do you hate?
2. What do you want for your birthday?
3. How many languages do you understand?
4. Do you have any pets? Talk about them.
5. What do you remember about being a child?
6. What do you think about the *Portrait* project?

Remember!

There are some verbs which are normally only used in the simple form, e.g. *like*, *love*, *hate*, *want*, *understand*, *remember*, *need*, *prefer*, *know*, *mean*, *sound*, *think* (have an opinion), *have* (possession).
I **know** that man.

- Use some of the verbs to make sentences of your own.

Grammar extra p127

Writing

Features of interviews

> In an **interview**, one person asks questions and the other one answers.

▶ **The people in an interview**

The person who asks the questions is the **interviewer**. The person who answers is the **interviewee**.

ACTIVITY
In the magazine article on page 9:
Who was the interviewer? _____
Who was the interviewee? _____

▶ **Interview questions**

The interviewer asks the interviewee for information. The questions often begin with question words:
What …? When …? Where …? Which …? Who …? How …?

ACTIVITY
Look at Jack's profile. There are eight pieces of information.
Write the question for each piece of information.

Profile

1	name:	Jack
2	age:	12
3	lives in:	West Hill, Hampton
4	sister:	Laura, aged 15
5	school:	West Hill Academy
6	interests:	swimming music
7	likes:	beach holidays talking to people Chinese food
8	dislikes:	long car journeys too much homework

Questions

1. _____
2. _____
3. _____
4. _____
5. _____
6. _____
7. _____
8. _____

▶ **Layout**

An interview is **set out like a play**. Look at this extract from the magazine article.
The names of the interviewer and interviewee are on the left. The words that they say are on the right.

Patsy: Which school do you go to?
Laura: I go to West Hill Academy.
Patsy: Have you got any brothers or sisters?
Laura: Yes, I've got one brother, Jack.

Writing

Writing together

> Patsy is interviewing Holly. As a class you are going to use the information below to write up the interview.

1 Read Holly's personal profile.

name:	Holly
age:	14
lives in:	Hampton town centre
brother:	Micky, aged 9
sisters:	Nancy, aged 9; Tammy, aged 6
school:	Central High School
interests/hobbies:	design (especially clothes), doing puzzles and quizzes
likes:	fashion, shopping
dislikes:	cold weather (especially wet, cold weather), too much homework

2 Things to think about.

For Patsy, the interviewer:
- Use the questions you wrote on page 14.
- Use the information in Holly's profile to write extra questions.
- Write the questions in full sentences.

For Holly, the interviewee:
- Use the information in Holly's profile to write her answers to Patsy's questions.
- You can use extra information about Holly in her answers. What did she say on pages 9 and 13?
- Write the answers in complete sentences.

What do you like designing?

I love … I hate …

> **Remember!**
> - Set out the interview like a play.
>   Patsy: *What's your name?*
>   Holly: *My name's …*
> - Use the question words on page 14.

3 Write the interview.

Individual writing WB p9

Writing together: an interview

Listening and speaking

Conversation practice

1 Jack and Ross are talking. Look at the pictures and the words in the box. What do you think they are talking about?

| live | have got | interested in | good at | like | dislike |

2 🎧 1.03 Listen to Jack and Ross. Were you right?

3 🎧 1.03 Listen again. In what way does Ross's family differ from Jack's? In what way are Jack's interests similar to Ross's?

4 Talk to your friends. Find out about each other. Start like this:
Do you live in an apartment or a house?

Listening comprehension

1 🎧 1.04 Listen to Ross talking about his family. Write the family members he mentions.

_____ _____ _____ _____ _____

2 🎧 1.04 What are their jobs or what do they want to be? Listen again. Tick the correct pictures.

      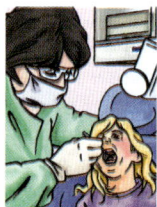  

☐ ☐ ☐ ☐ ☐ ☐ ☐ ☐ ☐

3 Talk about Ross's family.

Individual speaking

You are going to talk about your family. **WB p10**

City life 2

Check-in

Many cities are beautiful and interesting places. Sometimes they are crowded and noisy.

If you live in a city, do you like it? Why? / Why not?
If you don't live in a city, would you like to? Why? / Why not?
What cities have you visited?
List three cities you would like to visit. Say why.

You are going to read a story that is set in a city. It is about a boy called Philippe.

Reading

- The story is about something that happened to Philippe in **the past**. The writer uses the **past tense**.
- These words are in the story.

    dusty   fume   scent   drift   disguise
    cascade   spurt   chariot   mingle   broad

What do they mean? Check in your dictionary.

- The story **describes** the city square. The writer uses **adjectives**.

List five adjectives to describe a city.

- The writer describes what Philippe could **see**, **hear** and **smell**.

What can you see, hear and smell in the area where you live?

Vocabulary and spelling

- Learn **descriptive words** and **phrases**.
- Learn more about **suffixes** and **prefixes**.
- Learn when to **double consonants** before suffixing.

What is a suffix? List two.

Grammar

- Practise the **past simple** and **past continuous**.
- Practise **used to**.
- Practise when to use **make** or **take**.

Writing

- Learn about the writing **features of a descriptive text**.
- Write descriptions of the city square:
    - at night
    - in the rain.

Listening

- Holly and Ross's **presentation** of a castle.
- Jack and Ross's **conversation** remembering primary school.
- Jack's grandmother talking about her childhood.

What do you remember best about your primary school?

Speaking

- Talk with a partner about **your old primary school**.
- Tell the class about **a family member's childhood**.

Reading

The man at the fountain

Philippe was standing by his cousin's newspaper stall when he noticed the thief. Philippe knew he was a thief because his picture was in the newspapers. In fact, his picture was in every one of the newspapers that his cousin was selling at this very moment.

The square was bustling on this hot afternoon. Several stalls were selling cold drinks and snacks. People were sitting in the shade of the trees around the edge. Cooing pigeons strutted hopefully around the benches.

Buses with dusty windows were cruising around the square. They wove their way through the never-ending flow of traffic. Now and again, one stopped under the trees. Its engine hummed noisily as the doors hissed open. Blue-grey fumes rose into the air. Their oily smell mixed with the scent of roses that drifted from the flower seller's stall. Waiting passengers pushed their way onto the bus while others left it and hurried away across the square.

Nobody was taking any notice of the thief but Philippe did not stop watching him. He was difficult to recognise. He did not look exactly like his pictures because he was in disguise, but Philippe knew it was him. The police were looking for this man all over the city and now, here he was, just a few metres from the newspaper stand.

He was standing at the fountain in the middle of the square. He was almost hidden by a group of tourists with clicking cameras. They chatted and laughed as they took their photos. The square was famous for the fountain. Travellers to the city always took photos of the fountain with its beautiful statues and cascades of tinkling water. It was made from white marble that glistened like Arctic ice. In the four corners were huge, leaping fish. Water spurted from their gaping mouths and splashed into the pool. In the centre of the pool two powerful, galloping horses were pulling a magnificent chariot that was driven by a warrior of ancient times.

The thief was mingling with the tourists who were throwing seeds to the pigeons and photographing the elegant buildings around the square. Philippe thought about getting closer. He took a few steps forward.

"Hey!" Philippe heard his cousin's voice. "Aren't we going to the match? I'll finish here soon."

Philippe nodded and looked back at the man who was sliding a small camera from his pocket. He took several photos of the square. While Philippe was watching, he realised that one building particularly interested the thief. It had six white columns at the front. Broad steps led up to the massive, wooden doors and a blue and gold flag was flying above the vast entrance. It was certainly a beautiful building and a good one to photograph. It used to belong to a duke. Now, it was the city bank.

Philippe frowned and stared harder at the man. Just then, the group of tourists hurried away towards their bus. Startled pigeons took off in a cloud of grey. The thief was suddenly alone.

As if he felt Philippe's eyes on him, the man turned towards the fountain. An ice-cream seller pushed his cart across the square and stopped in front of the fountain. Philippe could no longer see the man. When the ice-cream seller moved on, the man was gone.

Philippe frowned again. "Perhaps he knew I was watching him," he thought. Just then, Philippe spotted a movement among the trees at the edge of the square. The thief was darting towards the main street that led away from the square. It was at that moment that Philippe decided to follow him.

Reading: a descriptive narrative

Reading comprehension

1 **Choose the best words to complete the sentences.**

1 Philippe's cousin was a newspaper _____. a reporter   b seller   c reader
2 The bus fumes mixed with the scent of _____. a oil   b flowers   c roses
3 The thief was difficult to _____. a recognise   b watch   c notice
4 The square was famous for _____. a the statues   b the pool   c the fountain
5 The fountain was made from _____. a white marble   b white ice   c Arctic ice
6 The thief was interested in _____. a photography   b the bank   c the buildings
7 The tourists hurried away towards _____. a their bus   b the bank   c the main street
8 The thief was suddenly _____. a hidden   b gone   c alone

2 **Think about the answers to these questions. Discuss your ideas.**

1 Why was nobody taking any notice of the thief?
2 Why was the thief mingling with the tourists?
3 Why did Philippe not get any closer to the thief?
4 Why did Philippe frown when he saw which building interested the thief?
5 Do you think the thief knew Philippe was watching him? Why? / Why not?
6 Why do you think Philippe decided to follow the thief?

3 **Read these sentences from the story. Underline all the adjectives.**

'It had six white columns at the front. Broad steps led up to the massive, wooden doors and a blue and gold flag was flying above the vast entrance.'

Now do the following tasks.

1 Rewrite the sentences. Leave out all the adjectives.
2 Read the sentences. Does the description of the building sound different? How?
3 Find two adjectives in the sentences that mean almost the same. What do they mean?

4 **Scan the text and find:**

1 five things that were being sold in the square
   _____ _____ _____ _____ _____

2 four things that the tourists were doing
   _____ _____ _____ _____

3 three animals
   _____ _____ _____

4 three vehicles
   _____ _____ _____

Your views

- Was Philippe right to follow the thief? Why?
- If you were Philippe, what would you have done?
- Was the man in the square definitely the thief in the papers? How do you know?

Working with words

A Language development
Adjectives: the present participle

1 Underline the present participle in this sentence.

The horses were galloping.

Read these sentences.

The horses were galloping. They crossed the valley quickly.

- These two sentences can be made into one sentence by using the present participle as an adjective.

The galloping horses crossed the valley quickly.

- The adjective describes the horses. A separate sentence about the horses' action is not needed.

2 Read these noun phrases from the text.

> gaping mouths   waiting passengers
> cooing pigeons

3 Read these pairs of sentences. Discuss how to write them as one sentence using the phrases in Activity 2.

1 The passengers were waiting. They pushed their way onto the bus.
2 The pigeons were cooing. They strutted hopefully around the benches.
3 Water spurted from their mouths. Their mouths were gaping.

You can check your answers in the text.

B Making new words
More about root words, suffixes and prefixes

- A root word cannot be broken into parts.
  e.g. *square   bus   stall   drink*
- Other words are made up of a root word with a **suffix** added.
  e.g. *power + ful* → *powerful*
       watch + ing → *watching*
- Some words have a beginning added in front of the root word. This is called a **prefix**. The prefix makes a new word.
  e.g. *un + usual* → *unusual*
- Other words contain a root word with both a prefix and a suffix added.
  e.g. *re + view + ing* → *reviewing*

1 Read this example. Complete the sentence.

disappeared The root word is _____;
            the prefix is _____; the suffix is _____.

C Spelling
Doubling before suffixing

> - If a root word ends in a single consonant with a single short vowel sound before it, and the suffix begins with a vowel, we usually double the consonant letter.
>   e.g. *trav**el**   trav**eller**   trav**elled**   trav**elling***

1 Write the past tense of these verbs. Then write the verbs next to the correct definitions.

quarrel _____   cancel _____
refer _____

1 to stop or end something _____
2 to mention someone or something _____
3 to have an argument _____

- In the adverb below, the consonant suffix -y sounds like the vowel sound ee so the consonant *l* is doubled.
  graceful   gracefully

Look out!
*gallop   gallo**p**ing*

Some words don't follow the rules.

- In words with the stress on the first syllable and ending consonant + *er* /ə/, the weak *r* does not count as a consonant.
  e.g. *cover   cove**r**ed*

Working with words: present participle as adjective; prefixes, suffixes; doubling before suffixing

Grammar

1 **Read.**

When Philippe **walked** into the square that afternoon, he **saw** that it **was bustling** with visitors. Some **were taking** photos of the magnificent fountain in the middle of the square. Some **were buying** cool drinks from the stalls around the edge. Others **were sitting** on benches in the shade of the trees.

Philippe **was making** his way across the square towards his cousin's newspaper stand when he **saw** the thief. The man **was wearing** a disguise but Philippe **recognised** him immediately. He **was mingling** with the tourists and taking photos of the square. While Philippe **was watching** him, the man **pointed** his camera at one of the elegant buildings and **started** to photograph it. That building **was** the bank!

2 **Answer these questions.**
1. Was the square empty or busy?
2. What were the tourists in the square doing?
3. What was the weather like? How do you know?
4. What was Philippe doing when he saw the thief?
5. What do you think the thief was wearing?
6. What was the thief doing?
7. What did the man do while Philippe was watching him?
8. What did Philippe think that the man was planning?

3 **Ask and answer. Use the past simple.**
1. Philippe – drive – into – square?
   A: Did Philippe drive into the square?
   B: No, he didn't.
2. What – Philippe – see?
3. Where – visitors – sit?
4. How – fountain – look?
5. Philippe – recognise – thief?
6. What – man – start to do?
7. What – Philippe – think?

4 **Cover the text. Correct these sentences.**
1. Few tourists were visiting the square.
2. Some people were sitting under the trees to escape the rain.
3. Others were buying hot drinks.
4. Philippe was mingling with the tourists.
5. Philippe's cousin was buying newspapers in the square.
6. The thief was drawing a picture of the square.

5 **Join the sentences. Use the words in brackets.**
1. Philippe entered the square. He saw a crowd of visitors. (when)
2. Philippe was watching the tourists. He spotted the thief. (when)
3. Philippe was crossing the square. He noticed the man. (while)
4. Philippe watched the man carefully. He was taking photos. (while)

6 **Write and talk. Answer the questions. Then compare your answers with those of your friends.**
1. While you were coming to school today, what did you see?
2. When you arrived at school, what did you do?
3. What were you doing when your teacher came into the classroom?

> **Remember!**
> - Use the past simple for actions which were completed in the past.
>   Philippe **entered** the square.
> - Use the past continuous for actions which continued for some time in the past.
>   The man **was taking** photos.
> - You can use both tenses in one sentence. Use *while* or *when*.
>   While Joe **was watching** TV, the telephone **rang**.
>   Joe **was watching** TV when the telephone **rang**.

- Think of more sentences using the past simple and the past continuous with *while*.

Grammar in use

1 Listen and read.

Laura: Are you ready? Can you remember your words? Action!
Holly: Hi there! Ross and I are outside Hampton Castle, the oldest building in our town.
Ross: Parts of the castle are almost 1,000 years old.
Holly: It **used to be** the home of the Duke of Hampton, one of the wealthiest men in the country.
Ross: The castle **used to stand** outside the town but over the years the town has grown.
Holly: So now the castle is in the centre of town.
Ross: Look at the strong stone walls and the small windows with their iron bars.
Holly: Hampton Castle also **used to be** a prison.
Laura: Don't forget to say when.
Ross: It was a prison for 300 years, until the middle of the last century.
Holly: And as many as 200 prisoners **used to live** and **work** in the building.
Ross: Today Hampton Castle welcomes different kinds of visitors.
Holly: Part of the castle is a museum and part of it is a hotel.
Ross: Inside the castle walls there are shops, restaurants and cafés.
Holly: Years ago, when people walked through the dark prison gates, they **used to feel** sad, depressed, angry and scared.
Ross: Yes, the castle **used to be** a gloomy, frightening place.
Holly: But today the atmosphere is very different. People love coming here. It's lively, colourful and lots of fun.
Ross: It's one of the most interesting and enjoyable places to visit in our town.
Laura: Great! You were brilliant! Well done!

Portrait Project
Place of interest: the castle
Video clip
Talking: Ross and Holly
Filming: Laura

2 Answer these questions.

1. When was Hampton Castle built?
2. Who used to live at the castle?
3. Where did the castle use to stand?
4. Where does it stand now? Why?
5. What did the castle use to be at one time?
6. How many prisoners used to live and work there?
7. What is the castle today?
8. How has the atmosphere changed over the years?

3 Change the sentences. Use *used to*.

1. The castle stood outside the town.
   The castle used to stand outside the town.
2. It belonged to the Duke of Hampton.
3. The castle always felt gloomy and depressing.
4. Nobody enjoyed visiting the castle.
5. Few tourists came to our town but these days there are many.
6. The town was poor but now it is wealthy.

4 Talk about it. Think about your town or city. Compare the present and the past.

1. Did it use to be bigger or smaller? Richer or poorer? Cleaner or dirtier?
2. What has changed? Have any buildings disappeared? What did there use to be?
3. What is new? What didn't you use to have in your town or city?

Remember!
Use *used to* for actions which:
- happened regularly in the past but not now.
  *Joe **used to walk** to school but now he goes by bus.*
- continued for some time in the past but not now.
  *Joe **used to like** football but now he prefers basketball.*

- Think of some more sentences using *used to*.

Grammar extra p127

Writing

Features of descriptive writing

> An important part of a writer's job is to **describe** things so the reader can imagine the scene where the story is set.

▶ **Past tenses**

Most stories are about something that happened in the past. The writer uses **past tenses**.

> The square **was bustling** on this hot afternoon.

> Blue-grey fumes **rose** into the air.

ACTIVITY

Find the past tense of these verbs in the story extract on pages 18–19.

Past simple:
1 to notice   2 to hurry
3 to know   4 to glisten
5 to weave

Past continuous:
1 to stand   2 to mingle
3 to sell   4 to dart
5 to sit

▶ **Aspects of the scene**

The writer chooses to describe various **aspects** of the scene:

the square: stalls   people   pigeons   the buses: windows   engines   fumes
the fountain: statues water   the building: columns   steps   doors   flag

▶ **Adjectives**

Adjectives are very important in descriptions.

> **cold** drinks and snacks   **dusty** windows   **beautiful** statues

ACTIVITY

Find **adjectives** in the extract that describe the following:
1 flow of traffic   2 smell   3 water   4 marble   5 horses   6 chariot

▶ **Adjectival phrases**

Adjectival phrases help the reader to imagine the scene.

> He was almost hidden by a group of tourists **with clicking cameras**.

> … a **blue and gold flag** was flying above the vast entrance.

▶ **Similes**

Similes can be very useful for making a description interesting.

> The fountain 'was made from white marble **that glistened like Arctic ice**'.

ACTIVITY

Think of **similes** you could use to describe:
1 the pigeons   2 the horses   3 the flag

▶ **See, hear, smell**

Descriptions not only describe what you can **see**. They also describe what you can **hear** and **smell**.

see: blue-grey fumes   hear: cooing pigeons   smell: scent of roses

ACTIVITY

In the extract find other **descriptions** of:
1 something you can see   2 something you can hear   3 something you can smell

Writing

Writing together

> In the story extract, the **setting** is a busy, noisy square during the day. As a class you are going to imagine the next part of the story takes place at night and write a description of the same square.

1 Think about the square at night.
- What does the square look like at night?
- How is it different from during the day?

2 Make notes on what you could **see**.
- Is the newspaper stall open or closed?
- Are there lots of buses or a few?
- Are the pigeons looking for food? Have they left the square?
- Is the fountain on or off? Is it dark or lit up?
- Are there lots of people or a few? What are they doing?
- Is the bank open or closed?

3 Make notes on what you could **hear**.
- traffic?
- voices?
- music?

4 Make notes on what you could **smell**.
- food?
- traffic fumes?

5 Write your **description** of the square at night in three paragraphs.

Paragraph 1: What it looks like.
Paragraph 2: What sounds there are.
Paragraph 3: What smells there are.

> Here are some useful **adjectives** you could use:
> shining   deserted   dark   empty   quiet   lonely   gloomy
> eerie   silent   shadowy   grey   peaceful   spooky

Individual writing WB p17

Writing together: a description **25**

Listening and speaking

Conversation practice

1 Jack and Ross are talking. Look at the pictures and the words in the box. What do you think they are talking about?

used to   go   favourite   like   hate   wear   play

maths
sport
English
music
science

2 🎧 1.07 Listen to Jack and Ross. Were you right?

3 🎧 1.07 Read the phrases in the box. Then listen again and spot the phrases.

How about you?   Really?   Poor you!   Wow!   Lucky you.

4 Talk to a friend. Talk about your old primary school and what you used to do when you were children. Use some of the phrases above if you can. Start like this:

Which primary school did you use to go to?

Listening comprehension

1 🎧 1.08 Listen to Jack's grandma. She is talking about her childhood.

2 🎧 1.08 Listen again and write T (true) or F (false).
  1 Jack's grandma used to live in the city. ___
  2 There were three children in the family. ___
  3 They used to spend a lot of time at the beach in summer. ___
  4 At weekends they used to sail to the island for a picnic. ___
  5 In winter the weather was often stormy. ___
  6 Jack's grandma didn't use to watch TV. ___
  7 She used to talk to her friends on her mobile. ___
  8 She had a happy childhood. ___

3 Talk about Jack's grandma's childhood.

Individual speaking

You are going to talk about the childhood of an older member of your family.   **WB p18**

Life at the edge

Check-in

Some people and animals live in parts of the earth where special skills and knowledge are needed to survive. However, present changes threaten the future of many of them.

What do you know about the Arctic Ocean?
What is a desert? Are all deserts hot?
How many deserts there in the world?
Find out the names of five deserts.

You are going to read information about endangered animals in the north.

Reading

- The **information** text is about polar bears and sea otters.
- It tells you **how they live** and **what threatens** them.
- It is set out in a **clear order** in **paragraphs**.
  What is a paragraph?

- These words are in the text.
  climate   threat   survive   reproduction   mammal
  extinct   pollution   industry
  What do they mean? Check in your dictionary.

Vocabulary and spelling

- Learn words to do with **animals** and **habitat**.
  What is a habitat?

- Learn about **suffixes** *-al* and *-y*.
- Learn about spelling **words with** *ei / ie*.

Grammar

- Practise **future meanings** with *will / going to*.
- Practise the **present continuous for future meaning**.
- Practise **phrases with** *catch*.

Writing

- Learn about the features of **note taking** and **drafting**.
- **Use notes** to write **information** about:
  - the sea otter
  - the polar bear.

Listening

- Laura, Jack and Holly's **discussion** of future plans using the present continuous.
- Laura and Ross's **conversation** about their future plans.
- Laura's **presentation of** a future weekend trip.

Do you make plans for the future?
Do you discuss them with friends? Your parents? Anyone else?

Speaking

- Talk with a friend about **future plans**.
- Present your **future plans** to the class.

What do you like to do at the weekend?

27

Reading

Endangered animals in the north

The polar bear

The future for polar bears is uncertain. The climate is changing. Every spring, the Arctic ice melts earlier and every summer there is less ice. The habitat of the polar bears may disappear. Nobody knows if they will survive.

Habitat

winter — summer

Polar bears live all round the Arctic, in northern Canada, Alaska, Greenland, Norway and Russia. In winter, ice covers the Arctic Ocean. The sea water around the land freezes, too. Polar bears hunt for food on the sea ice. In summer, when the sea ice melts, they live on the land but there is little food for them. They wait for the autumn when the sea freezes and they can go hunting again.

Appearance

Polar bears are the largest kind of bear. The male is about 2.5m tall and weighs around 500kg. The female is smaller, about 2m tall and weighs about 250kg. Their thick, white fur insulates them from the cold. Their feet are large and furry. They can walk across the snow easily. They can swim well, too, because their feet are partly webbed.

Diet

Polar bears hunt the seals that live under the ice in the Arctic Ocean. Seals make holes in the ice and they come up to breathe. The polar bear waits patiently by the hole. When the seal comes up, the polar bear tries to seize it in its powerful jaws.

Reproduction

In the winter, female bears make dens under the deep snowdrifts. Here the cubs are born. The mother bear keeps them warm and fed for several months without ever leaving them. When they are bigger, they go outside. The mother bear teaches them to hunt on the ice floes.

Threats

Loss of sea ice because of climate change is the main threat to polar bears, but pollution from industry and oil spills also threaten them. In Russia, a new Arctic Park has been created. Here, polar bears will live in safety, protected from harmful industrial activity.

Look at Nature

Animals in danger — This month, we're taking a look at the smallest sea mammal in the world.

The sea otter

Sea otters live in the North Pacific Ocean. There used to be hundreds of thousands of sea otters but almost all of them were hunted and killed for their fur. The sea otter was nearly extinct and only 1,000–2,000 were left. A hundred years ago, hunting sea otters was banned. Now there are more than 100,000. Read these facts about the sea otter.

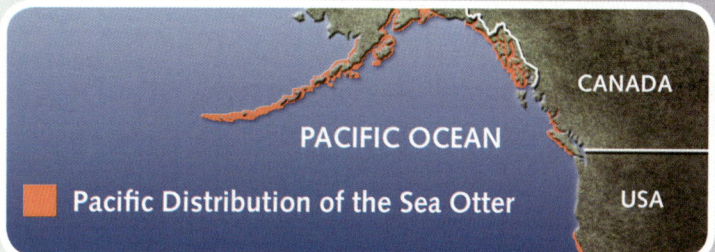
Pacific Distribution of the Sea Otter

Sea otters live near rocky coasts of the North Pacific and stay about 1km from the shore. They do not have dens on land and they can spend their entire lives in water. They sleep on the sea and eat there, too.

The sea otter has thicker fur than any other animal. The outer fur is waterproof. The soft fur underneath stays dry and protects the otter from the cold water. Otters are between 1m and 1.5m long and weigh from 20kg to 40kg. The females are smaller than the males. The otters' back feet are fully webbed and they can swim well underwater.

Sea otters dive to find food. They have long whiskers that help them to find their prey in dark water. They can lift boulders on the sea floor and search for sea creatures underneath them. They eat snails, crabs and shellfish. They use stones as small tools. They hit the shellfish with a stone to get them off the rocks.

Sea otters often sleep at sea in large groups of 10–100. They float on their backs and hold each other's paws to make a 'raft' and keep the group together.

Otter pups are born at sea. The mother floats on her back with her newborn pup on her chest. A young pup's fur has so much air in it that it bobs safely on the surface like a plastic ball and is safe from drowning.

The biggest threat to sea otters is oil spills. If a sea otter is covered in oil, its fur cannot keep it warm and it dies of cold. Thousands died in 1989 when an oil tanker spilled 40 million litres of oil into the sea.

Look at Nature – News just received!

Next year, more oil fields are opening in the North Pacific region. More ships will carry oil across the sea, so there is a greater chance that another accident will happen. The future of the sea otter is not guaranteed.

Reading comprehension

1 **Answer these questions.**
1. What is the Arctic Ocean like in winter?
2. Where do polar bears live in a) the winter? b) the summer?
3. How are polar bears insulated from the cold?
4. What animal do polar bears hunt on the sea ice?
5. Where has a new Arctic Park been created?
6. Why were sea otters hunted by people?
7. Where do sea otters spend their lives?
8. How big and how heavy are sea otters?
9. What food do they live on?
10. What happens to a sea otter if it is covered in oil?

2 **These words are subheadings in the text. Match them to the correct definition.**

   diet   threats   appearance   reproduction   habitat

1. where something lives _____
2. how something looks _____
3. what an animal or person eats _____
4. possible dangers _____
5. how an animal produces its young _____

3 **Think about the answers to these questions. Discuss your ideas.**
1. Why might the habitat of the polar bears disappear?
2. Explain how polar bears catch seals.
3. Why do you think an Arctic Park has been created in Russia?
4. What does that suggest about other parts of the Arctic?
5. Was it a good idea to ban the hunting of sea otters? Why? / Why not?
6. Why is the future of the sea otter not guaranteed?

4 **Match these words from the text to the correct definition.**

   webbed   survive   climate   floe   entire   waterproof   float   guarantee   pollution

1. the weather during different seasons _____
2. to continue to live _____
3. a large area of ice floating on the ocean _____
4. all of _____
5. having skin joining the fingers or toes _____
6. to be held up by water or air _____
7. dirt and rubbish in the environment _____
8. not letting water pass through _____
9. to promise that something is certain _____

Your views
- What facts about the polar bear most surprised you?
- What facts about the sea otter were most interesting?
- Which information was easier to read and understand: the polar bear or the sea otter? Why?

Working with words

A Making new words

Adjectives with the suffix -al

- Some nouns can be made into adjectives by adding -al.
  industry
  industr**al**
  industr**ial** activity

Here, the polar bears will live in safety, protected from harmful industrial activity.

1 Read these adjectives ending -al. Write the root word under the adjective.

1 musical   2 natural   3 seasonal
_____ _____ _____
4 coastal   5 continual   6 factual
_____ _____ _____

2 These adjectives also end -al. Complete them. Read them.

1 fin__ __   2 intern__ __   3 norm__ __
4 electric__ __ 5 comic__ __   6 sever__ __

3 Write next to these definitions the correct adjective from this page ending in -al.

1 funny _____   2 usual _____
3 near the shore _____   4 last _____
5 true _____   6 a few _____
7 happening all the time _____

Adjectives with the suffix -y

- Some nouns can be made into adjectives by adding the suffix -y.
  rock
  rocky
  rocky coast

Sea otters live near rocky coasts of the North Pacific.

Watch your spelling! Check in a dictionary!

4 Make these words into adjectives by adding -y.

1 fur _____   2 dust _____
3 dirt _____   4 powder _____
5 smoke _____ 6 nut _____
7 star _____   8 hand _____

B Spelling

Words with ei / ie

- When the sound is ee, the rule is:
  i before *e*, except after *c*.

Look at Nature — News just recei**ved!**
Next year, more oil fie**lds are opening.**

- We use ei when the sound is not ee.
  e.g. w**ei**gh *The male w**ei**ghs around 500kg.*

1 The sound in these words is ee. Complete them.

1 gr__ __f   2 rec__ __ve   3 ch__ __f
4 th__ __f   5 br__ __fcase

2 Match each word in Activity 1 next to the correct definition.

1 to get _____
2 the most important person in a large group of people _____
3 a person who steals _____
4 bag to carry papers _____
5 sadness _____

3 The sound in these words is not ee. Complete them. Use them to answer the question.

h__ __ght   w__ __ght

How tall and how heavy is a female polar bear?

Look out!

Spelling rules are helpful but some words do not follow them.

s**ei**ze

fr**ie**nd

Grammar

1 **Read.**

In three days' time, two 4x4s **will set out** from Sapporo on the Japanese island of Hokkaido. On board **will be** a team of wildlife experts, photographers and film-makers. They **will travel** two hundred kilometres to the south-east coast of Hokkaido where they hope they **will catch** a glimpse of one of the rarest Japanese mammals – the sea otter.

The team **is going to spend** a month among the rocks and cliffs around Cape Erimo, the otters' favourite location. They **are going to count** the otters and **observe** their behaviour. They **are going to film** the otters and other wildlife in the area. "It**'s going to be** very hard work," said Professor James Ball, the leader of the team, "but we're looking forward to it."

2 Answer these questions.

1. When will the team set out?
2. Who will be in the team?
3. Where will they travel to?
4. What do they hope they will see?
5. How long are they going to spend on the coast?
6. What are they going to do there? (Find three things.)

3 Talk about it. What do you think? Give reasons for your answers.

1. Will the journey to the coast be tiring? Why? / Why not?

 *I think …*

 *I don't think …*

2. How long will the journey take?
3. Will they catch a glimpse of the sea otters?
4. What other creatures will they see?
5. Will they enjoy their month at the coast?
6. How will they feel at the end of their trip?

4 Ask and answer about the team's plans. Use *going to*.

1. they – have – a holiday?
2. How hard – they – work?
3. How long – they – spend – on the coast?
4. What – they – observe?
5. What – they – film?
6. they – count – the otters?

5 Talk about your own plans.

1. What are you going to do after school today?
2. What are you going to do tomorrow?
3. What are you going to do next summer?
4. What are going to do when you leave school? Are you going to study or get a job? What are you going to study? / What job are you going to do?

Remember!
Use *will* + verb for actions which will happen in the future.
The concert will take place on Saturday.
Use *be going to* + verb:
- when talking about plans and intentions.
 John is going to be a doctor.
- when a situation in the present means that an action is sure to happen in the future.
 Look at those black clouds! It's going to rain.

- Think of some more sentences using *will* and *going to*.

Grammar in use

1 🎧 1.10 Listen and read.

Laura: The river's so beautiful. I love it.
Holly: Me, too! They**'re starting** boat trips next month.
Laura: It's a pity there aren't any boats for our photos.
Jack: Never mind. I'll take a photo of the bridge … Oh, no!
Holly: What's the matter?
Jack: It's the camera. There's something wrong with it.
Laura: You're joking!
Jack: No, honestly. It's not working.
Holly: Well, we'll have to find another camera and come back tomorrow.
Jack: No, we can't. Laura and I **are going** to London tomorrow.
Laura: What about the day after tomorrow?
Holly: That's no good for me. My cousin**'s coming** over. I**'m meeting** her in the morning and she**'s staying** all day.
Jack: This is ridiculous! We've got to take these photos!
Laura: Give me the camera … Oops!
Jack: Well, now it *is* broken. You're so clumsy.
Laura: It wasn't my fault!
Jack: Wait a minute! It's working!
Holly: Thank goodness for that! Now let's take these photos of the river …

Portrait Project
Local beauty spot:
the river
Laura, Jack and Holly
Take photos

2 Answer these questions.

1 Why have Jack, Holly and Laura come to the river?
2 Are there any boats on the river?
3 When are the boat trips starting?
4 Why can't Jack take a photo?
5 Can they take the photos tomorrow? Why not?
6 What is Holly doing the day after tomorrow?
7 Do you think Laura is clumsy?
8 Was it good or bad to drop the camera? Why?

3 Look at these notes in Holly's diary. Then ask and answer.

Jack and Laura	Monday	London
	Wednesday	dentist
	Sunday	revise for exam
Ross	Tuesday	basketball
	Friday	help father
	Saturday	swimming – Sports centre
Me	Tuesday	meet cousin
	Thursday	shopping centre
	Sunday	work on project

1 Holly – Thursday
   A: What's Holly doing on Thursday?
   B: She's going to the shopping centre.
2 Ross – Tuesday
3 Jack and Laura – Monday
4 Holly – Tuesday
5 Ross – Saturday
6 Jack and Laura – Sunday
7 Holly – Sunday
8 Ross – Friday
9 Jack and Laura – Wednesday

Remember!
You can use the present continuous for future events which are the result of plans or arrangements in the present.
We**'re having** pizza for dinner tonight.
My cousins **are coming** to stay next weekend.
Harry **is taking** his driving test next week.

• Think of some more sentences using the present continuous to talk about future events.

Grammar extra p127

Grammar in use: present continuous for future events; Grammar extra: phrasal verbs with *catch*

Writing

Study skills: note taking and drafting

You are going to write a **report** on an endangered species.

Stage 1 – research
Research is finding out about the subject. You can use books, magazines and the internet.

Stage 2 – making notes
Don't just copy out of books. Make **notes** from what you have read.
Let's look at the notes you could make for the polar bear.

> polar bear – around Arctic / N. Canada / Alaska / Greenland / Norway / Russia
> winter = land & sea ice / summer = land
> **reproduction:** winter = female build den under snow / cubs (how many?) / mother looks after them = several months
> **size:** male 2.5m tall / female 2m tall
> **threats:** future uncertain / climate change = less ice / pollution from industry – oil spills / Russia has Arctic Park to protect polar bears
> **hunts:** seals through holes in ice / fish / birds
> **appearance:** largest species of bear / white fur = thick / insulates from cold / feet – large / furry / webbed
> **weight:** male 500kg / female 250kg

Stage 3 – ordering your notes

Look what the notes tell you about the polar bear. Put the notes in this **order**:

1. where it lives, e.g. Arctic
2. what it looks like, e.g. white fur
3. what it eats, e.g. seals
4. its young, e.g. cubs
5. threats, e.g. climate change

Stage 4 – writing the first draft

Using only the notes, here is a paragraph on the polar bears.

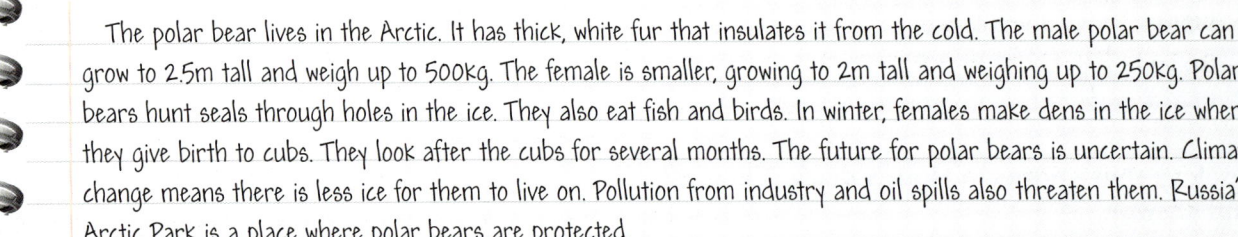
> The polar bear lives in the Arctic. It has thick, white fur that insulates it from the cold. The male polar bear can grow to 2.5m tall and weigh up to 500kg. The female is smaller, growing to 2m tall and weighing up to 250kg. Polar bears hunt seals through holes in the ice. They also eat fish and birds. In winter, females make dens in the ice where they give birth to cubs. They look after the cubs for several months. The future for polar bears is uncertain. Climate change means there is less ice for them to live on. Pollution from industry and oil spills also threaten them. Russia's Arctic Park is a place where polar bears are protected.

Stage 5 – proofreading

Checklist:
- Have you put in all the important information?
- Are your spellings correct? Check any you are unsure about.
- Is your punctuation correct? Have you put in all the capital letters and full stops?
- Make any corrections.

Stage 6 – the final draft

Give your work a title. Write it out neatly.

Writing

Writing together

> As a class you are going to use **notes** to write a paragraph about the sea otter.

1 Read these **notes** about the sea otter.

```
sea otter - North Pacific / rocky coasts / 1km from shore /
can spend entire life in water
threats: hunted / killed for fur / oil spills / nearly extinct /
hunting banned / now more than 100,000
breeding: pups born at sea / mother floats with pup on chest /
pup's fur has air in it = safe from drowning
weight: 20kg 40kg
hunts: snails / crabs / shellfish / uses stones to get shellfish
off rocks / long whiskers help find prey in dark water
size: between 1m 1.5m long / female smaller than males
appearance: thicker fur than other animals / fur = waterproof /
soft fur underneath = stays dry - protects from cold /
webbed feet / long whiskers
```

2 Use the **notes** to write a paragraph about the sea otter.

Remember!
- Order your notes.
- Write the first draft.
- Proofread.
- Give your work a title.
- Write it out neatly.

Individual writing WB p27

Listening and speaking

Conversation practice

1. Laura and Ross are talking. Look at the pictures and the words in the box. What do you think they're talking about?

   weekend   doing   playing   going   having   swimming
   looking   seeing   going shopping

2. 🎧 1.11 Listen to Laura and Ross. Were you right?

3. 🎧 1.11 Listen again. Spot two things that Laura and Ross are each doing at the weekend.

4. What are you doing this week? Make a list of the things you are doing. Talk to a friend about their plans. Start like this:

   So … what are you doing this week, (name)?

Listening comprehension

1. 🎧 1.12 Look at the pictures below and then listen to Laura. She's talking about the sights which she's going to see in London.

2. 🎧 1.12 Listen again. Number the pictures from 1–6 in the order in which Laura mentions them.

3. Talk about Laura's trip to London.

Individual speaking

You are going to talk about your future plans. **WB p28**

Advertisements 4

Check-in

Advertisements are all around us. You can see them in the street. You can see them in magazines.

Think of three more places where advertisements appear.
Why do you think people use advertisements?
What kind of advertisements do you look at most often?
How can the word advertisement be shortened?

You are going to read an advertisement for an Adventure Sports Centre.

Reading

- An advertisement **persuades** us to buy something, visit somewhere or do something.
- It is designed to be **eye-catching**.
- An advertisement often uses only a **few words** but the words and pictures are carefully chosen.
- These words are in the advertisement.

> **exhilarating   unique   half price   reduction**
> **benefit   unforgettable   skills   challenge**

What do they mean? Check in your dictionary.

Vocabulary and spelling

- Learn words to do with **advertising** and **persuasion**.
- Learn about **words ending -ent / -ence** and **-ant / -ance**.
- Learn about spelling **words with ou / oo**.

Think of three adjectives to describe something you think is really good.

Grammar

- Practise the **present perfect**.
- Practise the **present perfect** with **just / yet** and **for / since**.
- Practise **phrases with bring**.

Writing

- Learn about the writing features of **advertisements** and **persuasive** texts.
- Write persuasive **leaflets** for:
  - a basketball match
  - a school sports competition.

Listening

- Laura and Ross **presenting** a sports centre and a team captain.
- Laura and Jack's **conversation** about tasks completed or not done.
- An **interview** with a basketball team captain.

Have you played any sports this week?

Speaking

- Talk to a friend about tasks you **have done** or **haven't done** yet.
- Tell the class about **your tasks for this week**.

Do you keep a checklist of what you've done or not done?

Reading 🎧 1.13

It's **Thrilling** ➡ It's **Exhilarating** ➡

It's **Unique!**   It's the ...

ADVENTURE

Aerial runway

This isn't just sport – it's adventure sport!

Vertical slide

I've just been down the vertical slide – woweee! Unbelievable! Unforgettable! Unmissable!

Join the Adventure Sports Club

Get these great benefits:
- 10% off entry to the Adventure Sports Centre on any day
- half price entry on selected weekends
- one free training session a year
- 15% reduction on group bookings of 10 or more
- free Adventure Sports Club T-shirt
- free Adventure Sports Club bag
- automatic membership of the Sports Park Complex
- members-only evening sessions

I've been a member for a year. It's fantastic. You can do all the adventure sports and you can do lots of other sports, too!

Contact us:
The Adventure Sports Centre
The Sports Park Complex
North Avenue

Phone: 3385 00100
email: info@asc.com
www.asc-spc.com

We are open:
Tuesday – Sunday
10.00 – 6.00

7.00 – 9.00
members only

38 Reading: an advertisement

Reading comprehension

1 **Answer these questions.**
1. What is the advertisement for?
2. How many sports are illustrated?
3. Which activities might make you feel like a bird? Why?
4. What can you join at the Adventure Sports Centre?
5. How many benefits are there for club members?
6. How many ways can you contact the centre? What are they?
7. How many days a week is the centre open?
8. How far is the centre from the motorway?
9. What three things does the centre provide to help with safety?
10. What two words describe the trainers at the centre?

2 **Match these adjectives to the correct definition.**

| exhilarating   unbelievable   electrifying   unforgettable   unique |

1. cannot be forgotten _____
2. making you feel extremely excited _____
3. the only one and different to all the others _____
4. cannot be believed _____
5. making you feel happy and full of energy _____

3 **Talk about the words in the advert.**
1. a What form of the verb are three of the four adjectives at the top of the advertisement? _____
   b Why do you think this was chosen for these three adjectives?
   c Why do you think the fourth adjective is different? Why is it illustrated with a lion?
2. a The girl who has just been down the vertical slide uses three adjectives. What prefix do they all begin with? _____
   b Why do you think these words with the same beginning were chosen?
3. a Scan the text. Find seven verbs in the imperative.
   _____ _____ _____ _____ _____ _____ _____
   b Why does the advert use verbs in this form? What effect do they have on the reader?

4 **Think about the answers to these questions. Discuss your ideas.**
1. Do you think the membership benefits for the Adventure Sports Club are good? Why?
2. Why do you think safety is included in the advert?
3. Why do you think the advert tells you about the trainers?
4. What protective clothing do you think you need for these activities?
5. What kind of people do you think the advert is aimed at?

Your views
- Which activities would you like to do? Why?
- Which activities would you not like to do? Why?
- Which one do you think would be easiest? Which would be the most difficult?
- Have you ever done an activity like any of these? What was it?

Working with words

A Making new words

Words ending -ent / -ence

- Some adjectives that end -ent can be made into nouns by changing the ending to -ence.
  e.g. confident adj.   confidence n.
- Confidence is an **abstract noun**. You cannot hear, see, smell, taste or touch confidence. It is something you think or feel.

Learn new skills with **confidence**.

1 These adjectives end -ent. Complete the words and write the abstract nouns under the adjectives.

1 differ____   2 sil____   3 excell____
_____   _____   _____

4 evid____   5 pati____   6 obedi____
_____   _____   _____

2 Write the abstract nouns again next to the correct definition. Check in your dictionary.

1 proof; the sign or signs that something has happened _____
2 the act of doing as you are told _____
3 the ability to wait calmly without giving up _____
4 complete quiet _____
5 belief in your own ability to do something _____
6 the opposite nature of two things _____
7 the very good quality of something _____

Words ending -ant / -ance

- Some adjectives that end -ant can be made into nouns by changing the ending to -ance.
  e.g. distant adj.   distance n.

Find us: a short **distance** from the motorway.

3 These adjectives end -ant. Complete the words and write the abstract nouns.

1 import____   2 brilli____   3 eleg____
_____   _____   _____

4 defi____   5 ignor____   6 reli____
_____   _____   _____

4 Write the abstract nouns again next to the correct definition. Check in your dictionary.

1 not knowing anything _____
2 beauty and grace _____
3 how much something matters _____
4 the support needed from something or someone _____
5 opposition; disobedience _____
6 the shining nature of something _____
7 how far away something is _____

B Spelling

Words with ou / oo

- In some words ou and oo have the same short u sound: c**ou**ld   b**oo**k

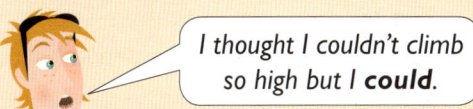

I thought I couldn't climb so high but I **could**.

15% reduction on group **bookings**

These words have the short u sound.
sh**ou**ld   w**ou**ld   l**oo**k   h**oo**k

- In some words, ou and oo have the same long oo sound.
sw**oo**p   gr**ou**p

swoop like a bird   15% reduction on **group** bookings

These words have the long oo sound.
s**ou**p   b**oo**t   r**ou**te   p**oo**l   w**ou**nd   r**oo**t   thr**ou**gh

1 Complete these words with ou or oo. Decide whether the vowel sound is long or short. Write short or long vowel after each word.

1 t__ l _____   2 t__ k _____
3 w__ l _____   4 y__ __ _____
5 w__ ld _____   6 w__ nd _____

Grammar

1 **Read.**

The Adventure Sports Club welcomes two new members!

Jason Darby **has been** a keen sportsman for most of his life. He **has tried** the usual sports like swimming, tennis and football and some more unusual ones, too, such as kite surfing, wakeboarding and parachute jumping. Unfortunately, Jason **has** recently **broken** his arm so he must wait a few weeks before he tries skydiving in our famous wind tunnel. Get well soon, Jason!

Miranda John is also no stranger to danger. She **has climbed** mountains in South America and **has dived** deep in the Pacific Ocean. She **has played** basketball for her country and **has won** a silver medal at the Olympic Games™. She **has tried** many sports but she **hasn't tried** our famous vertical slide! Welcome to the club, Miranda!

2 Read and say *Yes, No* or *Perhaps*.
1. Jason Darby has been interested in sport for a short time.
2. He has tried many different sports.
3. This is the first time he has broken his arm.
4. Miranda John is a keen sportswoman.
5. She has not tried any dangerous sports.
6. She is looking forward to the vertical slide.

3 Ask and answer.
1. How long – Jason – be – interested – sport?
   A: How long has Jason been interested in sport?
   B: He has been interested in sport for most of his life.
2. How many – sports – he – try?
3. he – do – parachute jumping?
4. he – break – leg?
5. Where – Miranda – dive?
6. she – play – football?
7. Miranda and Jason – win – medals?

4 What has happened? Look at the pictures and make sentences. Use the present perfect.

Ouch!

Uh oh!

Where's my purse?

5 Write and talk. Answer the questions. Then discuss your answers.
1. How many foreign countries have you visited? Where have you been?
2. What films have you seen recently?
3. What is the best book that you have read?
4. What lessons have you had in school today?

Remember!
We use the present perfect:
- for actions that have happened during a period of time leading up to the present. Exactly when the actions happened is unknown or unimportant.
  *Miranda and Jason **have tried** many sports.*
- when an action happened in the past and we can see the result of that action now.
  *Look! Someone **has broken** the window.*

- Think of some more sentences using the present perfect.

Grammar in use

Portrait Project
Sports centre
Ross, Jack and Laura
Report on basketball team
Interview players

1 Listen and read.

Laura: You know how the camera works, don't you, Jack?
Jack: Yes, of course! Stop making such a fuss!
Laura: OK. Here goes ... Today we're at Hampton Sports Centre. It's only **been** open **since** January but it's already become an important part of our town.
Ross: If you're keen on sport, this is the place to come. You can swim and dive, play badminton or tennis, do trampolining or gymnastics ...
Laura: There's even a climbing wall if you're feeling brave!
Jack: **Have** you **tried** it **yet**, Laura?
Laura: Er ... no ...
Ross: But we're here today because Hampton Sports Centre is the home of our hugely successful basketball team: the Hampton Hippos!
Laura: We're all very excited because the Hippos under-21 team **has just won** the semi-final of the National Basketball Competition.
Ross: And we're going to speak to their captain, Luke Jones.
Laura: And here he is! Congratulations, Luke. That was a great match.
Luke: Thanks. The team's **trained** really hard **for** months and months. I think we deserved to win.
Laura: The finals are next month, aren't they? We can't wait for you to bring back that silver trophy.
Luke: Oh! Don't speak too soon! We **haven't won** it **yet**!

2 Answer these questions.

1. How long has the sports centre been open?
2. What has it become?
3. What sports can you do there? Name three.
4. Has Laura tried the climbing wall yet?
5. Have the Hippos just won the National Basketball Competition?
6. How hard have they trained?

3 Make sentences. Use the present perfect and *for* or *since*.

1. sports centre – be – open – January
   The sports centre has been open since January.
2. players – train – hard – weeks and weeks
3. Luke Jones – play – basketball – ten years
4. Ellen – live – Hampton – eighteen months
5. castle – stand – hill – ancient times
6. Jack – have – a cold – last Saturday

4 Look!

Have you done all your homework yet?

Yes, I have.

No, I haven't done it yet.

Write five questions with *yet*. Ask and answer with your friends.

5 Change the sentences. Use *just*.

1. Someone stole my bag a moment ago.
   Someone has just stolen my bag.
2. The team won the competition a few minutes ago.
3. A famous actor opened the new sports centre a short time ago.
4. The girls finished their project a short while ago.
5. Joe spoke to his teacher a moment ago.

Remember!
We use the present perfect:
- for states or actions which have happened in a period of time leading up to the present.
  Use *since* + a definite time.
  Use *for* + a period of time.
  My uncle **has lived** in Paris **since** 2005.
  Sally **has been** ill **for** two weeks.
- with *just* for actions which happened a very short time ago.
  Harry **has just gone** to school.
- with *yet* in questions and negative sentences.
  Have you **finished** your homework **yet**?
  I **haven't written** my composition **yet**.

- Think of some more sentences using the present perfect with *since*, *for*, *just* and *yet*.

Grammar extra p128

Grammar in use: present perfect with *for*, *since*, *just* and *yet*; Grammar extra: phrasal verbs with *bring* 43

Writing

Features of persuasive writing

> **Advertising** is used to **persuade** us to visit somewhere, buy something or do something. The advert about the Adventure Sports Centre is trying to persuade us to join the centre.

▶ **Powerful words**

Words can be very powerful. They can be used to **persuade** us. The Adventure Sports Centre is described as:

> thrilling   exhilarating   electrifying

ACTIVITY

Imagine you did the following activities. What **powerful words** would you use to describe them to a friend?
1. skydiving
2. bungee jumping
3. the vertical slide

▶ **Alliteration**

Sometimes writers use words that begin with the same sound. This is called **alliteration**. It grabs the reader's attention.

> **Un**believable! **Un**forgettable! **Un**missable!

ACTIVITY

Complete each sentence by adding a word beginning with the **same sound** as the underlined word.
1. I had a <u>wonderful</u>, _____ day at the sports centre.
2. The bungee jump was a <u>terrific</u>, _____ experience.
3. The <u>fantastic</u>, _____ climbing wall is my favourite.

▶ **Information**

People need to be given **information** about the sports centre.

> We are open: Tuesday – Sunday
> Phone: 3385 00100

▶ **Layout**

The way the advertisement **looks** is very important. It is laid out using different:

colours
fonts
headings
illustrations

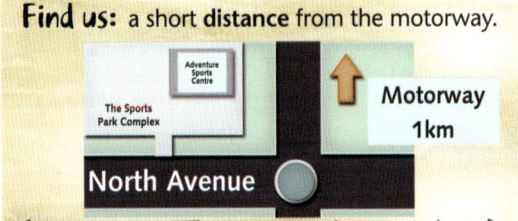

▶ **Quotes**

Quoting what people who have visited the sports centre **think** can be very persuasive.

I thought I couldn't climb so high but I could! What an incredible day.

Writing

Writing together

> The Hampton Hippos have reached the finals of the National Basketball Competition. As a class you are going to design a **handout** advertising the finals and persuading people to come and support the team.

1 Read this factfile about the Hampton Hippos.

> **Under-21 team**
>
> captain = *Luke Jones*
>
> first time they have entered the National Basketball Competition
>
> beat the Roaring Rhinos in the semi-final – *score* **16 / 9**
>
> playing the Trent Town Tigers in the final

You can include some of this information in your handout.

2 Think of a **heading** for your handout.
- What is the first thing people will read on the handout?
- What size of letters will you use?
- What colour will the heading be?

3 Discuss what **information** people will need to have about the competition. Think about:
- date
- time
- venue
- who the Hippos are playing
- ticket prices

4 Think about **persuasive language**. You want people to read the handout and buy tickets – not just throw it away!

powerful words: *thrilling / exciting / not to be missed*
alliteration: *Hampton Hippos in hunt for trophy / fantastic final*

5 Make up a **quote** from someone who saw the semi-final and can't wait for the final!

6 Come up with a design for your handout. Remember that how an advert **looks** is important. Think about:
- use of colour
- illustrations
- size of letters

Individual writing

Listening and speaking

Conversation practice

1 Jack and Laura are talking. Look at the pictures and the words in the box. What do you think they are talking about?

> yet   just   done   finished   started   revised
> phoned   sent   emailed   tidied

2 🎧 1.15 Listen to Jack and Laura. Were you right?

3 🎧 1.15 Read the phrases in the box.
Then listen again and spot the phrases.

> How about you?   What a fuss you're making!
> Poor you!   Oh, really?   What a mess!

4 Talk to a friend about this week's school work. What have you done? What haven't you done yet? What other things haven't you done yet? Make a list. Start like this:

Hey (name)! I haven't done my (subject) homework yet. Have you?

Listening comprehension

1 🎧 1.16 What do you remember about Luke Jones? Listen to Laura's interview with Luke. Then say if you remembered correctly.

2 🎧 1.16 Listen again and answer these questions.
   1 What have the Hippos just won?
   2 What was the score?
   3 Has the team trained hard for a short time or a long time?
   4 How long has Luke played with the Hippos?
   5 How long has he been the captain of the team?
   6 How long has he played basketball?
   7 Why did he start playing basketball?
   8 Is Luke sure that the Hippos will win the final? What does he say?

Individual speaking

You are going to talk about what you have done this week and what you haven't done yet.

WB p36

Great lives 5

Check-in

Biographies are usually written about famous people. The person may have died a long time ago, quite recently or the person may still be living. Sometimes the person is not well-known at all.

> Have you read a biography? Who was it about?
> Think of three people you would like to know more about.
> Why do you want to know more about them?

You are going to read a short biography of a British queen.

Reading

- A biography is often written in the **past tense**.
- The **events** in the person's life are usually **told in the order** that they happened.
- A biography gives **details** of the person's **life**, **feelings** and **character**.

> A biography often begins with the date a person was born. When were you born?

- These words are in the biography.

  governess   lonely   request   guidance   devastated
  empress   expansion   obedient   harsh

> What do they mean? Check in your dictionary.

Vocabulary and spelling

- Learn words to do with **life events of a ruler**.
- Learn about the **suffixes -ment** and **-ness**.
- Learn about spelling **words with gu**.

Grammar

- Practise **comparative adjectives** and phrases: *as big as*.
- Learn the comparative structure: *not as big as*.
- Practise **superlative** and **irregular** adjectives.
- Practise phrases with *look*.

Writing

- Learn about the features of **biographical writing**.
- Write a **biography** of an English queen from **notes**.

> Can you name any English queens?

- Make your **own notes** and write a **biography** of a relative.

Listening

- **An interview** with a famous astronomer.
- Holly and Ross's **conversation** about favourite things to do.
- An astronomer's **description** of the night sky.

Speaking

- Talk with a friend about **favourite things to do**.
- Tell the class about **your best project**.

47

Reading

Victoria, Queen of the United Kingdom

Victoria's early life

Princess Alexandrina Victoria was born into the British royal family on 24th May, 1819. Her mother was extremely protective and the princess grew up under strict rules. She was never allowed to be alone. Her mother, her tutor or her governess was always with her. She shared a bedroom with her mother. In her playtime, her only friends were her dolls and her little dog, Dash. When she was older, she described her childhood as rather sad and lonely. At the age of seventeen she was introduced to a handsome young German, Prince Albert. She liked him at once but she was not yet ready to marry.

A new queen

The princess was 18 on 24th May, 1837. Less than a month later, her uncle, the king, died and she became queen on 20th June, 1837. Her first two requests were to have an hour by herself and to have her bed removed from her mother's room to a bedroom of her own. She did not want to be called Queen Alexandrina. Instead she asked for her second name, Victoria, to be used.

Marriage

Victoria was crowned on 28th June, 1838, and she made Buckingham Palace her home. Because she was not married, her mother also lived in the palace but Victoria often refused to see her. She met Prince Albert several times over the next two years. Finally, she asked him to marry her and their wedding took place on 10th February, 1840. Victoria adored her new husband from the start and she relied on him for advice and support in her role as queen. She had to meet the prime minister, listen to his ideas for government and make decisions about matters of state.

Family life

Their first child was born in November, 1840, and over the next seventeen years they had eight more children. Family life became important to Victoria. With Prince Albert's guidance she became a better daughter to her mother. When her mother died in March, 1861, Victoria was at her bedside. In December of the same year, Prince Albert died after a short illness and Victoria was devastated. She wore black for the rest of her life. She continued her government duties but she did not live in London. She stayed in her castles in the south of England and in Scotland. Because of this, she was not so popular as before. She was advised to be seen in public more often and gradually she appeared at more public events.

The British Empire

During Victoria's reign the British Empire expanded. Much of India came under British rule and from 1st May, 1876, Victoria was also named Empress of India. In her opinion, the expansion of the British Empire helped other countries and protected people from cruel rulers. Other countries did not have the same point of view and saw Britain as a threat. Britain was often at war for the Empire, which was more powerful than it had ever been before.

The Victorian period

Victoria's reign was known as the Victorian period. Family life was important to everyone. Bad behaviour was not allowed and children had to be obedient. It was a time of industrial progress. Factories, railways and bridges were built. Cities expanded greatly. For those who had good jobs and comfortable homes, life was pleasant, but for the poorer people who lived in the worst houses, life was hard. Work in the factories was exhausting and often dangerous. Many people spoke out against the harsh conditions and the well-known writer, Charles Dickens, wrote about them.

Final years

Victoria's reign of 63 years, 7 months and 2 days was longer than the reign of any king or queen before her. She had become immensely popular. Her children had married into European families and she had more than thirty grandchildren. She was known as 'the grandmother of Europe'. When she became ill and died on 22nd January, 1901, aged 81, the whole population was deeply saddened. She was buried next to her husband, Prince Albert.

Reading comprehension

1 Read the statements. Write *T* (true) or *F* (false). Correct the false statements.

1. The princess was always with her mother or her tutor or her governess. ___
2. When she was introduced to Prince Albert, she wanted to marry him. ___
3. One of her first requests was to have an hour in bed by herself. ___
4. After Victoria was crowned, she lived in Buckingham Palace. ___
5. After 1861, Queen Victoria wore black dresses every day. ___
6. From 1st May, 1876, Victoria was named Empress of Britain. ___
7. In the Victorian period, children did not have to do what they were told. ___
8. Factories were always a good place to work. ___
9. Queen Victoria was known as the 'grand old lady of Europe'. ___
10. She died and was buried next to her husband in 1901. ___

2 Who are these people? Match them to the descriptions.

a	tutor	1	a person who controls a country
b	governess	2	a woman who rules an empire
c	prime minister	3	the man who is married to a woman
d	husband	4	a woman who looks after and teaches children in their own homes
e	ruler	5	a person who teaches children in their own homes
f	empress	6	the leader of the British government

3 Think about these questions. Discuss your answers together.

1. Why do you think Victoria described her childhood as rather sad and lonely?
2. Why do you think Victoria sometimes refused to see her mother after she was queen?
3. Do you think Victoria made a wise choice in marrying Prince Albert? Why?
4. From what you have read about Victoria, what sort of person do you think she was? Think of at least three adjectives to describe her character.
5. Why do you think she had become so popular by the end of her reign? Think of three reasons.

4 Scan the text and find:

1. three people, one of whom was always with Victoria as a child
   _____   _____   _____
2. two requests Victoria made as soon as she was queen
   _____   _____
3. the number of children Victoria and Albert had altogether _____
4. two people who died in 1861 _____   _____
5. three structures that were built in the Victorian period
   _____   _____   _____
6. the exact length of Victoria's reign _____

> **Your views**
> - Would you feel sad and lonely if you were brought up like Victoria? Why or why not?
> - Would you prefer to be born into an important family or an ordinary family? Why?
> - From what you have read, which of these words do you think best describes Victoria's life. Why?
>
> easy   sad
> lonely   busy
> successful

Working with words

A Making new words

The suffix -ment

> - A lot of verbs in English can be made into nouns by adding -ment.
>   govern govern**ment**
>   *She listened to his ideas for govern**ment**.*

1 Read these pairs.

1	agree	agreement
2	argue	argument
3	excite	excitement
4	equip	equipment
5	entertain	entertainment

Look what happens to argue when the suffix is added.

2 Write the nouns in Activity 1 next to the correct definition.

1 a discussion in which people have opposite views _____

2 a performance or presentation which is fun and interesting _____

3 special items necessary for a particular purpose _____

4 when people have the same views about something _____

5 a happy and lively feeling _____

3 Change these verbs to nouns by adding -ment.

1 govern_____   2 move_____
3 disappoint_____   4 pay_____
5 advertise_____   6 appoint_____
7 arrange_____   8 state_____
9 announce_____   10 measure_____

Use your dictionary to check meanings ...

... and spellings!

4 Write two other nouns that end in the suffix -ment.

_____   _____

Use your dictionary if you need to.

The suffix -ness

> - Some adjectives can be made into nouns by adding -ness.
>   ill ill**ness**
>   *Prince Albert died after a short ill**ness**.*

5 Read these pairs.

1	kind	kindness
2	sick	sickness
3	gentle	gentleness
4	naughty	naughtiness
5	ugly	ugliness

6 Use each noun in a sentence of your own.

7 Write the nouns from these adjectives.

weak	tidy	dark
_____	_____	_____
lazy	narrow	useful
_____	_____	_____

B Spelling

Words with gu

> - In most words beginning gu + vowel, you can't hear the *u*.
>   *guidance*
>   *With Prince Albert's **guidance** she became a better daughter to her mother.*

1 Write these words in alphabetical order.

> guide   guitar   guess   guest
> guard   guilty   disguise   guarantee

_____
_____

Check any new words in your dictionary.

2 Choose three words from Activity 1 and use them in sentences of your own.

_____
_____
_____

Working with words: suffixes -ment / -ness; words with gu-

Grammar

1 **Read.**

Victoria had a rather sad and lonely childhood. Her mother was strict and protective and her governess and tutor were **as strict as** her mother. Victoria was **not as free as** other children. However, her life became **happier** when, at the age of seventeen, she was introduced to a German prince named Albert. Albert was a few months **younger than** Victoria and very handsome. They married four years **later**.

During Victoria's reign the British Empire became **larger** and **more powerful than** it had ever been before and Victoria was a much loved queen. However, when Albert died at the early age of 42, Victoria was devastated. She left London and rarely appeared in public. For a time she was **not so popular as** she had been before. She died in 1901. Her reign was **longer than** that of any king or queen before her.

2 Read the sentences and write *T* (true) or *F* (false).

1. Victoria had a very happy childhood. ___
2. Her governess was not as strict as her mother. ___
3. Victoria was not as free as other children. ___
4. Victoria was happier after she met Albert. ___
5. Victoria was younger than Albert. ___
6. The British Empire became smaller during Victoria's reign. ___
7. After Albert's death Victoria was more popular than she had been before. ___
8. Victoria reigned for a long time. ___

Correct the false sentences.

3 Ask and answer. Start your answers with *Yes, No* or *I'm not sure if …*

1. Victoria – free – other children?
   A: *Was Victoria as free as other children?*
   B: *No, she wasn't as free as other children.*
2. Victoria's governess – strict – her mother?
3. Albert – old – Victoria?
4. Victoria – intelligent – Albert?
5. Albert – popular – Victoria?
6. Albert – young – Victoria?
7. Victorian children – well-educated – today's children?

4 Make true sentences. Compare.

1. Victoria – Albert – young
   Albert was younger than Victoria.
2. Victoria's married life – her childhood – happy
3. As a girl, Victoria – other children – protected
4. Albert – Victoria – old
5. Victoria – kings and queens today – powerful
6. London today – London in Victorian times – big

5 Talk about towns in your country.

Where do you live?
Choose another town in your country and compare it with your home town.

Here are some adjectives which you can use. Choose different adjectives if you want.

> big small beautiful interesting busy
> noisy quiet dirty clean hot
> cold exciting peaceful

Make notes. Then talk with your friends.

> **Remember!**
> When you compare two items, …
> - if they are the same, use *as … as*.
>   *Lily is **as** tall **as** her brother.*
> - if they are different, use *not as … as* (or *not so … as*).
>   *They are not **as tall as** their father.*
>   or use *-er than* or *more … than*
>   *Ben is old**er than** his sister.*
>   *Anna is **more intelligent than** Ben.*
>
> Use *-er than* with:
> - one-syllable adjectives, e.g. *big, small*.
> - some two-syllable adjectives, e.g. *noisy, busy, quiet*.
>
> Use *more … than* with:
> - some two-syllable adjectives, e.g. *peaceful, harmless*.
> - adjectives with three or more syllables, e.g. *dangerous, complicated*.
>
> - Make more sentences with *as … as*, *-er than …* and *more … than*.

52 Grammar: comparative adjectives

Grammar in use

Portrait Project
Famous local person: Professor Magnus Bolt, TV astronomer
Holly – interview
Ross – draw portrait

1 Listen and read. (1.18)

Holly: Professor, when did you first become interested in astronomy?

Professor: Well, one of my **earliest** memories is seeing a shower of shooting stars. I was about five or six at the time. I thought it was **the most magical** thing I had ever seen.

Holly: How beautiful!

Professor: Yes, it was. I couldn't stop talking about it so my father bought me a telescope. It was **the best** present I've ever received.

Holly: Were you good at science at school?

Professor: Yes, I was. I was terrible at history and not much **better** at geography. I was even **worse** at languages! And as for art, that was **the worst** of the lot! No, the only subject I was interested in was science – and astronomy in particular.

Holly: How do you become an astronomer?

Professor: Learn to love the night sky. That's the first step. Get to know the stars, the constellations and the planets. And buy a good telescope!

Ross: Can we see your telescope, Professor?

Professor: Of course! It's a bit bigger than the one that I had when I was five!

2 Answer these questions.

1. What is Professor Bolt's earliest memory?
2. How does he describe it?
3. What was the best present he has ever received?
4. At school was Professor Bolt good or bad at science?
5. Was he better or worse at languages?
6. What was his worst subject?

3 Think about it. Talk about it.

1. What subjects are you good at?
2. Are you bad at anything?
3. Are you better at art or science?
4. Are you worse at maths or languages?
5. What's your best subject?
6. What's your worst subject?

4 Complete the sentences with *the most* and the words in the box.

| beautiful | delicious | dangerous |
| difficult | fascinating | expensive |

1. I think Chinese is …
   I think Chinese is the most difficult language in the world.
2. Gold is one of …
3. Many people believe that the white shark is …
4. Professor Bolt thinks that astronomy is …
5. Most people think that roses are …
6. Some people think that strawberries are …

Remember!
Superlative adjectives have two forms:
- *the* + adjective + *-est*: January is **the coldest** month.
- *the most* + adjective: This is **the most delicious** cake.

Use *the* + adjective + *-est* with:
- one-syllable adjectives, e.g. *hot, tall*.
- some two-syllable adjectives, e.g. *heavy, clever*.

Use *the most* + adjective with:
- some two-syllable adjectives, e.g. *polite, handsome*.
- adjectives with three syllables or more, e.g. *beautiful, astonishing*.

Don't forget the irregular adjectives:
good, better, the best; bad, worse, the worst

- Think of more sentences using *the* + adjective + *-est*, *the most* + adjective and the irregular adjectives.

Grammar extra p128

Grammar in use: superlative, comparative and irregular adjectives; Grammar extra: phrasal verbs with *look*

Writing

Features of biographies

> A **biography** is the story of a person's life written by someone else. People who write this type of book are called biographers.

▶ **Past tenses**

Biographies are often written about people who have died. They are written in **past tenses**.

> ... the princess **grew** up under strict rules.

> Her children **had married** into European families ...

ACTIVITY
Find five more examples of **past tenses** in the biography of Queen Victoria.

Princess Alexandrina as a child

▶ **Order**

Biographies usually begin with the person's **birth** and go through their life in **order**.

> Princess Alexandrina Victoria was born ... **on 24th May, 1819.**

> ... she became queen on **20th June, 1837.**

> Their first child was born in **November, 1840** ...

ACTIVITY
Find the **dates** when Victoria:
1 was crowned
2 got married
3 died

▶ **Facts**

Biographies give the **details** of a person's life – the **facts**.

> At the age of seventeen she was introduced to a handsome young German, Prince Albert.

> ... they had eight more children.

▶ **Character and feelings**

Biographies also tell us something about the **person's character and feelings**.

> ... she was not yet ready to marry.

ACTIVITY
Discuss what these quotes tell you about Victoria.
1 ... [was] to have an hour by herself
2 ... her mother also lived in the palace but Victoria often refused to see her
3 She saw the expansion of the British Empire as helping other countries and protecting people from cruel rulers.

Writing

Writing together

> The biography you have read is about Queen Victoria, Queen of the United Kingdom from 1837 to 1901. As a class you are now going to write a short biography of Elizabeth I, Queen of England from 1558 to 1603.

1 Read these notes about Elizabeth's life.

- 1533 - born at Greenwich, near London, 7th September, 1533
  Father = King Henry VIII   Mother = Queen Anne Boleyn
  Henry disappointed the baby was not a boy
- Education = Latin and Greek
- Leisure: riding / archery / card games / dancing / needlework
- 1553 - Elizabeth's half sister, Mary, became queen
  Elizabeth imprisoned in the Tower of London for 2 months
- 1555 - allowed back to live with the Queen
- 1558 - became Queen at age 25
- Very popular / clever / vain / liked to be the centre of attention
  Refused to marry and share her power
- During reign she was interested in:
  exploration - encouraged sailors such as Drake and Raleigh to explore the world
  the arts - very fond of the theatre - saw plays by Shakespeare, Marlowe and Johnson
  her people - passed laws to help the poor
- 1603 - died on 23rd March at 3am aged 70
  Buried in Westminster Abbey in London at the end of April
  Ruled for 45 years

Queen Elizabeth I

Henry VIII

Shakespeare

2 Use the notes to write a short biography of Queen Elizabeth in three paragraphs.

Paragraph 1: Elizabeth's birth and early life
Paragraph 2: Elizabeth as Queen
Paragraph 3: Elizabeth's death

Individual writing   WB p45

Listening and speaking

Conversation practice

1. Holly and Ross are talking. Look at the pictures and the words in the box. What do you think they are talking about?

> like   prefer   better   the best   more exciting   funnier
> the most interesting   favourite   brilliant   fantastic

2. 🎧 1.19 Listen to Holly and Ross. Were you right?

3. 🎧 1.19 Read the phrases in the box. Then listen again and spot the phrases.

> Hmm …   Let me see …   Well, to be honest …   Of course!   Fantastic or what?

4. Talk to a friend about books, films, computer games, music and TV programmes. Start like this:

What sort of books do you like reading, (name)?

Listening comprehension

1. 🎧 1.20 What do you remember about Professor Bolt? Listen to a part of his TV programme. What is he talking about this week?

2. 🎧 1.20 Listen again.
   1. Number these things in the order in which Professor Bolt mentions them.
      a comet ___   a shooting star ___   a planet ___   stars ___   the moon ___
   2. How does Professor Bolt explain these things?
      a a constellation   b a full moon   c a comet
   3. Would you like to watch Professor Bolt's TV programmes? Why? / Why not?

Individual speaking

You are going to talk about the best project that you have done in school.

WB p46

What a character! 6

Check-in

Stories, plays and films all have characters. Interesting characters make events more real.

Make a list: a cartoon character, an ugly character, a funny character, a hero, a scary character.
Who is your favourite character?
Which character do you love to hate the most?

You are going to read a story with characters.

Reading

- Stories are usually written in **past tenses**.
- A **descriptive story** uses carefully chosen words to create an impression of the **characters**.
- Authors have several ways of presenting a character. Here are two:
  - how the person **looks** • how the person **behaves**

Stories are fiction. What does fiction mean?
What does that tell you about the characters?

- These words are in the story.
  waft   screwdriver   scrutinise   expression   forehead
  eyebrow   chin   concentration

What do they mean? Check in your dictionary.

Vocabulary and spelling

- Learn words to do with a **person's appearance** and a craftsman's **tools**.

Name three different tools you already know.

- Learn about words **ending -ate** and **word classes**.
- Learn about spelling **words with silent c**.

Grammar

- Practise **articles** *a/an*, *the*; no article.
- Practise **verb + infinitive**: *I want to visit Georgia*.
- Learn **verb** + *ing*.
- Practise **phrases with** *stand*.

Writing

- Learn features of **character writing** from:
  - how the person **looks** • how the person **behaves**
- Write **descriptions** of characters from:
  - how they look • what they do.

Listening

- An **interview** with a factory worker.

What factories do you know about? What goods are made there?

- Laura, Ross, Holly and Jack discussing **jobs** they would like to do.
- A girl talking about the **career** she wants.

Speaking

- Talk with friends about **plans for jobs**.
- Tell the class about **your future career**.

Reading

Mr Duffy's workshop

Grandfather wanted George to go to Mr Duffy's house to collect a present. The present was for George's little cousin, Sally. "Mr Duffy phoned this morning," Grandfather told George. "He's finished. Would you mind going now?" George didn't mind going at all. He loved to go to Mr Duffy's house at any time. He loved talking to Mr Duffy about his work. Most of all, he was fascinated by Mr Duffy's tools.

A few minutes' walk brought George to a tall house. He knocked on the old wooden door. After a few moments, Mrs Duffy opened it. "Come along in, George," she said. "Mr Duffy is in the workshop." She walked ahead of George along a short passageway and stopped at the open kitchen door. George caught a glimpse of bowls of plums and peaches on the kitchen table. A delicious smell of simmering fruit wafted past his nose. Mrs Duffy pointed to an open doorway, where bright sunlight fell across the single step. "You know your way, don't you, George?"

George nodded. "Thank you, Mrs Duffy," he said.

George stepped into the small courtyard, brilliant with flowers cascading in streams of white, pink and crimson from pots on the window sills. In one corner a peach tree drooped its branches, laden with golden fruit. Near the tree, a door stood open. George crossed the courtyard and stepped inside Mr Duffy's workshop. This was one of George's favourite places in all the world and Mr Duffy was one of his favourite people.

Mr Duffy was leaning over his workbench. On the wall beside him, clean but well-used screwdrivers, chisels and pliers of varying sizes were ranged in neat racks alongside hammers and saws. Rows of tiny paint pots and varnish stood on narrow shelves with fine, delicate brushes in long plastic boxes and pots of screws and nails. Mr Duffy's glasses were perched on the end of his nose and he was looking carefully at a thick piece of wood. He ran his long fingers gently over the surface. He was frowning a little with an air of concentration. He scrutinised the wood for a few seconds then he stood up straight with an expression of satisfaction. At that moment, he noticed George and turned towards him with a welcoming smile.

The most striking thing about Mr Duffy was that he was extremely tall. The second most striking thing was that he was extremely thin. This always surprised George as he never came to the house without smelling something delicious cooking on the stove. He wondered how Mr Duffy stayed so thin when so much tasty food was produced from Mrs Duffy's kitchen. Mr Duffy peered at George over the rims of his glasses. He had a large nose above a pointed chin and a broad forehead with thick dark eyebrows. His short, greying hair stood straight up from his head. He seemed to George like a wise old bird, sharp-eyed and thoughtful. He always wore a long blue apron which made him look even taller and thinner. In the pocket was a short pencil, which he sharpened from time to time with a tiny penknife.

"Hello, George," said Mr Duffy.

"Hello, Mr Duffy," replied George.

Mr Duffy beckoned George to a table against one wall. This was the table where Mr Duffy put finished pieces of work. There was a large, polished box made of gold-coloured wood and a small round table with intricately carved legs. Beside the table was Sally's present. It was a small wooden boat. Across the middle of the boat were three little benches and each bench had three holes in. In each hole was a small round wooden sailor with a blue body, a round head and tiny sailor hat. They looked as though they were sitting on the benches. Mr Duffy lifted out one of the sailors and showed it to George. The sailor had dark hair, rosy cheeks and a curly moustache. He was winking in a very cheeky fashion. George laughed. He looked at the other sailors. All their faces were different. Some were old and some were young, but they all looked friendly and cheerful.

George grinned at Mr Duffy. "Sally's really going to love this," he said.

Reading comprehension

1 Answer these questions.
1. What did Grandfather want George to collect?
2. Why didn't George mind going to Mr Duffy's house?
3. What did George see on the kitchen table and what did he smell?
4. What things were growing in the courtyard?
5. What things were in Mr Duffy's workshop?
6. What was Mr Duffy doing when George went into the workshop?
7. What was Mr Duffy like? What did he wear?
8. How did he seem to George?
9. What three objects were on the table?
10. What was Sally's present?

2 Match the adjectives in the box to the nouns. Write the descriptive phrases.

rosy   tasty   sharp-eyed   neat   polished

1. _____ box
2. _____ man
3. _____ racks of tools
4. _____ cheeks
5. _____ food

3 Think about the answers to these questions. Discuss your ideas.
1. What do you think George liked about Mr Duffy's workshop?
2. Why do you think Mr Duffy was one of George's favourite people?
3. What sort of person do you think Mrs Duffy was? How do you know?
4. What sort of person do you think Mr Duffy was? How do you know?
5. Why do you think George felt that Sally would like the present?

4 Find each verb in the text. Read the whole sentence. Try to guess the meaning. Write the word next to the correct definition below.

a waft   b simmer   c droop   d lean   e scrutinise
f carve   g wink   h grin   i mind   j perch

1. to bubble gently over heat _____
2. to shut then open one eye very quickly while looking at someone _____
3. to make an object by cutting from wood or stone _____
4. to float in the air _____
5. to hang down _____
6. to bend the body in the middle _____
7. to look very carefully _____
8. to give a very big smile _____
9. to not want to do something _____
10. to sit on the edge or end of something _____

Reading the sentences that come before and after the target word can help you work out the meaning.

Your views
- Would you like to spend time in Mr Duffy's workshop? Why? / Why not?
- Do you think the present for Sally was a good one? How old do you think Sally was?
- Do you like objects that are made by a craftsman? Why? / Why not?

Working with words

A Making new words

Words ending -ate

1. Some words end -ate. Read these examples.

   delicate _____   intricate _____
   educate _____   illustrate _____
   fascinate _____   concentrate _____
   insulate _____   motivate _____
   separate _____   fortunate _____
   chocolate _____   celebrate _____

   You have already used some of these words in this book. Check the words you don't know in your dictionary.

2. The words in the list in Activity 1 belong to three different word classes. Write the classes.

   _____ _____ _____

3. Some of the words in the list belong in more than one class.

   I like chocolate and I love chocolate ice cream.
       ↑ (noun)   ↑ (adjective)

   Write *v.*, *adj.* or *n.* after the words in the list. Use a pencil. If you think a word belongs in more than one class, write both of them.

   Don't look in your dictionary.

4. Write words from Activity 1 next to the correct definition.

   1. to protect from extreme cold _____
   2. to place people or objects apart from each other _____
   3. to mark a particular event with special activities _____
   4. very lucky _____
   5. to interest greatly _____
   6. fine, thin, easy to break or damage _____
   7. complex in design _____
   8. to encourage and interest _____
   9. to inform and teach _____
   10. apart, different _____
   11. to draw pictures for a book or a piece of writing _____
   12. to give all one's thoughts and attention to something _____

5. Now check the word classes you wrote in Activity 1. Correct any you got wrong.

6. In Activity 4 you should have written one word twice. Which word can be used as an adjective or a verb? _____

B Spelling

Silent c

- In some words, *c* follows *s* and you can't hear the *c*.

Fascinating!

1. These words have a silent *c*. Read them. Write them under the correct picture.

   scissors   scent   science
   crescent   descend   ascend

   1 _____   2 _____   3 _____

   4 _____   5 _____   6 _____

2. Check you have spelled all the words correctly. Underline the silent *c* in each word.

Grammar

1 **Read.**

Grandfather wanted George to go to Mr Duffy's house to collect **a present**. **The present** was for George's little cousin, Sally. George was happy to go. He soon arrived at **a** tall **house** and knocked on **the door**. Mrs Duffy opened it and invited him in. In **the kitchen** George noticed **bowls** of **plums** and **peaches** on **the table**. **A** delicious **smell** of simmering **fruit** wafted past his nose.

Flowers filled **the** small **courtyard**. **The flowers** were white, pink and crimson. In one corner stood **an** old peach **tree** and near **the tree** was **a** small open **door**. It was **the door** to Mr Duffy's workshop. George stepped inside. Mr Duffy was leaning over his workbench. **Tools** were hanging on **the wall** behind him. **The tools** were well-used but clean.

2 **Answer these questions.**
1 Why did George go to Mr Duffy's house?
2 Who was the present for?
3 What did George see in the kitchen?
4 What could he smell?
5 What was the courtyard full of?
6 What colours were the flowers?
7 What kind of tree was there in the courtyard?
8 What was near the tree?
9 What did George see on the wall of the workshop?
10 Can you describe the tools?

3 **Remember!**
When you talk about something for the first time, use *a* or *an*. When you mention it again, use *the*.

Make sentences.
1 George – collected – present
   present – for – cousin
   George collected a present.
   The present was for his cousin.
2 George – arrived – tall house
   house – belonged – Mr Duffy
3 George – noticed – old tree
   tree – in – corner
4 Mrs Duffy – holding – bowl
   bowl – full – fruit

4 **Remember!**
We use *the* when we know there is only one of something.
*George knocked on **the** door.*

Find some more examples in the text above.

5 **Remember!**
- With plural nouns and uncountable nouns we use no article when we are speaking in general.
- When we are speaking about something specific, we use *the*.
  *I like **strawberries** but **the strawberries** that I bought aren't sweet.*
  *We can't live without **water**. **The water** in our river is polluted.*

Make sentences.
1 animals – the animals
2 music – the music
3 rain – the rain
4 sweets – the sweets
5 fruit – the fruit
6 trainers – the trainers

62 Grammar: articles (*a*, *an*, *the* and *zero article*)

Grammar in use

Portrait Project
Local industry:
Larkin's Leather
Jack and Laura interview
Sally Cooper

1 Listen and read.

Laura: Hampton isn't a big industrial town but there are some factories here and the oldest is Larkin's Leather. It was founded by Alfred Larkin in 1859.
Jack: Today we're talking to Sally Cooper, who works at the factory. Sally, do you **like working** at Larkin's Leather?
Sally: Yes, I do. It's a very friendly company.
Laura: What does the factory make exactly?
Sally: We make all kinds of high-quality leather goods: boots, shoes and sandals, suitcases, briefcases, handbags …
Jack: What are you making at the moment?
Sally: I'm **helping to make** some belts. I **need to be** very careful because the belts are for a top designer.
Jack: How many people work here?
Sally: There are fifty of us in the machine room. It's very noisy!
Jack: Do you work long hours?
Sally: Yes, we do but I **don't mind working** hard.
Laura: Are you **planning to stay** at the factory, Sally?
Sally: Well, I **enjoy working** here but I've **decided to go** to college. I **want to study** design and I've **managed to get** on a course which starts next September.
Jack: Well done! Good luck with that!
Sally: Thanks a lot! I'm **looking forward to trying** something new.

2 Answer these questions.

1. What is Sally helping to make at the moment?
2. Why does she need to be very careful?
3. What has she decided to do?
4. What does she want to study?
5. What has she managed to do?
6. What is she looking forward to doing?

3 Make sentences.

1. Sally – like – work – factory
   Sally likes working at the factory.
2. She – not mind – work – hard
3. She – good at – sew – leather
4. She – enjoy – make – high-quality goods
5. She – like – design – shoes and bags
6. She – look forward – start – college course

4 Ask and answer.

1. What – Sally – help – make?
   A: *What is Sally helping to make?*
   B: *She is helping to make some belts.*
2. Why – need – work – carefully?
3. she – plan – stay – factory?
4. What – want – study?
5. Where – decide – go?
6. manage – get on – course?

5 Think about it. Talk about it.

1. Think of at least three answers to each question. Make notes.
   • What do you love doing?
   • What do you hate doing?
   • What are you looking forward to doing?
2. Talk about your answers with your friends.

Remember!
- Some verbs are followed by the infinitive.
  e.g. *Sally **is planning to do** a design course.*
  need, want, plan, help, decide, manage + infinitive
- Some verbs are followed by the gerund.
  e.g. *She **doesn't mind working** hard.*
  like, hate, enjoy, mind, look forward to, be good/bad at, be interested in + gerund

• **Think of some more sentences using verb + infinitive and verb + gerund.**

Grammar extra p128

Writing

Features of portraying character

> **Characters** in stories have to be more than 'just a name'.
> We need to know what they look like and what sort of people they are.

▶ **Past tenses**

Stories are usually written in **past tenses**.

He **knocked** on the old wooden door.

Mr Duffy **was leaning** over his workbench.

ACTIVITY
Find five more examples of **past tenses** in the story.

▶ **Physical appearance**

The author tells us a lot about the character, Mr Duffy. She tells us about what Mr Duffy looks like – his **physical appearance**.

extremely tall   extremely thin

He had a large nose and a broad forehead …

ACTIVITY
Find **descriptions** in the story that tell you about:
1   his hair
2   his fingers
3   his eyebrows
4   how he was dressed

▶ **Personality**

The author tells us about what Mr Duffy did. This helps to understand what sort of person he is – his **personality**.
• We know he is tidy.

His tools were 'ranged in neat racks'.

• We know he takes pride in his work.

… he was looking carefully at a thick piece of wood.

ACTIVITY
Discuss what these sentences **tell you about Mr Duffy**.
1   'He was frowning a little with an air of concentration.'
2   'He scrutinised the wood for a few seconds then he stood up straight with an expression of satisfaction.'
3   'At that moment, he noticed George and turned towards him with a welcoming smile.'

Writing

Writing together

> In the story extract, the only thing we know about Mrs Duffy is that she is a good cook. As a class you are going to write a **description** of Mrs Duffy cooking in her kitchen.

1 **Mrs Duffy's appearance.** In pairs agree the answers to these questions.
   - Is she tall or small?
   - What colour is her hair?
   - Does she wear glasses?
   - Does she have a friendly face?
   - Does she smile?
   - Is she fat or thin?
   - What colour are her eyes?
   - Does she wear an apron?
   - Does she look bad-tempered?
   - Does she frown?

2 **Mrs Duffy's personality.** In groups, choose words from the boxes below, or use your own ideas.
   - How do you think she feels about her work?

     enjoys it   doesn't enjoy it   doesn't care

   - How does she measure the ingredients?

     carefully   carelessly   messily   neatly

   - How does she stir or chop?

     energetically   slowly   thoughtfully   clumsily

   - How does she keep her kitchen?

     tidy   untidy   clean   dirty

   - What does she do while she works?

     sings   whistles   mutters   stays silent

3 Write a **description** of Mrs Duffy cooking in her kitchen.

   Remember!
   - Use past tenses.
   - Use adjectives to describe Mrs Duffy's physical appearance.
   - Show her personality by describing how she cooks.

Individual writing

Listening and speaking

Conversation practice

1 Jack, Laura, Ross and Holly are talking. Look at the pictures and the words in the box. What do you think they're talking about?

> want   would like   decide   plan   need
> like   enjoy   love   hate   not mind   be used to

2 🎧 1.23 Listen to Jack, Laura, Ross and Holly. Were you right?

3 🎧 1.23 Read the phrases in the box.
Then listen again and spot the phrases.

> You mean …   How about you?   Well …   … something like that
> Really?   What about you?   Wait a minute!

4 Talk with your friends about your future career plans. Start like this:

(Name), what do you want to do when you leave school?

Listening comprehension

1 🎧 1.24 Listen to Jane Anderson. She is talking about her future career plans. What does she want to do when she leaves school? Why does she want to follow this career?

2 🎧 1.24 Read the sentences. Then listen again and write T (true) or F (false).

1 Jane has always wanted to be a vet. ___
2 When she was ten, she wanted to be a ballet dancer. ___
3 Jane has been interested in animals for a long time. ___
4 She needs to get good marks in her science exams. ___
5 She does not enjoy studying hard. ___
6 She will need to study at university for six years. ___
7 She wants to specialise in horses. ___
8 Jane has got a horse of her own. ___

Correct the false sentences.

3 Talk about Jane's past and future career plans.

Individual speaking

You are going to talk about your future career plans.   **WB p54**

This is what to do 7

Check-in

If you want to do something but you don't know how to do it, you have to follow instructions.

Have you made something from instructions? What?
Think of three people who give you instructions.
What things do they tell you to do?
Do you give instructions to anyone? Who?
What do you tell the person to do?

You are going to read the instructions for a recipe.

Reading

- The **recipe** is set out clearly. It tells you:
  - what you are going to make
  - what you need to make it
  - what to do.
- The sentences are **short** and **clear**.
- The sentences use **imperative** verbs.

Choose six verbs from this page. Write them in the imperative form.

- These words are in the recipe.
    fridge   fresh   ingredients   prepare   refrigerate
    crush   beat   fry

What do they mean? Check in your dictionary.

Vocabulary and spelling

- Learn words for **ingredients** and **cooking**.
- Learn about the **past participle** as an **adjective**.

What is the past participle of write?

- Learn about the **prefix pre-**.
- Learn about spelling **words ending -ture**.

Grammar

- Learn the **zero conditional**.
- Practise words and phrases about **amounts** of things.
- Learn and practise **phrases with turn**.

Writing

- Learn about the features of **writing instructions**.
- **Rewrite unclear instructions** to make them easy to understand.
- Write **clear instructions** from pictures.

Listening

- Laura, Jack, Holly and Ross's **discussion** of their presentation of the shopping centre for their project.
- Laura and Jack **talking about shopping**.
- **Conversations** from different shops.

Do you go to the shopping centre? How often?
Do you go shopping anywhere else? Where?

Speaking

- Talk with a friend about your **local shops**.
- Tell the class about your **favourite shop**.

Reading

Brilliantly Healthy Beefburgers

Try making these healthy burgers from these delicious fresh ingredients.

Ben's Brilliantly Healthy Beefburgers

Ingredients

a little olive oil
1 medium onion, finely chopped
2 garlic cloves, crushed
450g best minced beef
3 tbsp chopped fresh parsley or 3 tsp chopped thyme
1 small egg, beaten
1 tsp tomato sauce
salt and freshly ground black pepper

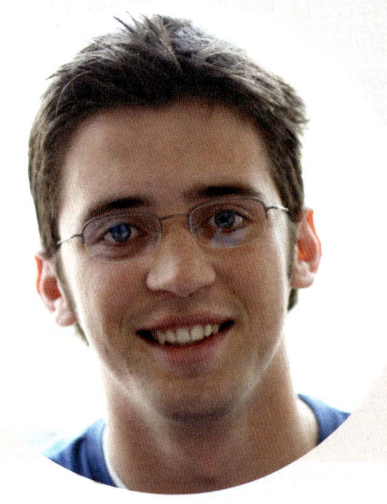

Method

1. Heat the oil in a pan, add the onion, garlic and some salt and fry gently until soft.
2. Take off the heat and put aside to cool.
3. Put the mince into a bowl and add the fresh parsley or thyme, egg, tomato sauce, a little salt and pepper, and the fried onion and garlic.
4. Mix the ingredients well with a fork.
5. Form the mixture into four burgers and refrigerate for five minutes. → **Tip:** If you refrigerate the burgers, they don't fall apart when you cook.
6. Meanwhile, prepare the rolls, salad filling, tomato ketchup and mayonnaise.
7. Preheat a frying pan and brush the burgers with a little oil.
8. Cook the burgers for three minutes on each side. Repeat until they are cooked. → **Tip:** The cooking time depends on the thickness of the burger.
9. Leave the burgers for one minute.
10. Put the burgers in the rolls with your salad and favourite sauces.

Serve the burgers with ...
4 soft rolls
tomato
lettuce
tomato ketchup
garlic mayonnaise

Choose a recipe – get cooking!

Then eat!

Bella's Brilliantly Healthy Beefburgers

First you cook some onion and garlic with a bit of salt in a pan with a little oil. You don't need much salt but remember to heat the oil before you start to cook. Carry on cooking until it is soft. Then stop cooking and let it cool down. Add an egg, tomato ketchup, salt and pepper to some minced beef. You can put them all in a bowl and also put in the onion and garlic mixture that you've just cooked. You need 450g of minced beef.

Tip If you haven't got any parsley, you can use thyme instead.

Tip I like lots of mayonnaise but I don't like a lot of tomato sauce.

If you add fresh herbs, the beefburgers taste better so I always do that.

Mix everything up in the bowl. You can use a fork to mix everything up or you could use a spoon. To make four beefburgers, you need to divide the mixture into four parts then use your hands to make four beefburgers. Put them in the fridge. Cut the rolls and get out your salad, tomato sauce and garlic mayonnaise. Now you can start cooking the beefburgers. Remember to heat the pan first. Before you cook them, brush some oil on them. Cook them on one side for three minutes then turn them over and cook them on the other side for three minutes. Then do it again. If the burger is thin, it takes less time to cook. If it is thick, it takes more time to cook. Put the burgers in the rolls with some salad and the sauces but leave them for a minute first.

Reading comprehension

1 Answer the questions. Note short answers.

A Ben's recipe

1 How does Ben show his ingredients?
2 How many steps are there in his method?
3 How much tomato sauce do you need?
4 How long do you put the burgers in the fridge for?
5 Why do you put them in the fridge?
6 What do you do with the frying pan before you start cooking the burgers?
7 How long do you leave the burgers for?

B Bella's recipe

1 How does Bella show her ingredients?
2 What must you do with the oil before you start to cook?
3 How much minced beef do you need?
4 Why does Bella add fresh herbs?
5 What does Bella not like a lot of?
6 How many burgers do you make?
7 What do you need to do with the burgers before you start cooking them?

2 Think about the answers to these questions. Discuss your ideas.

1 What are the two main differences between Ben's recipe and Bella's recipe?
2 Did you notice any other differences between the recipes?
3 Which recipe is easier to follow? Why?
4 Are Ben's tips helpful? Why? / Why not?
5 Are Bella's tips helpful? Why? / Why not?

3 Read the sentences. Match them to the pictures to put the sentences in the correct order.

_9_ Leave the burgers for one minute.
___ Put the burgers in the rolls with salad and sauces.
___ Prepare the rolls, salad and mayonnaise.
___ Form 4 burgers and put into the fridge for 5 mins.
___ Cook the burgers for 3 minutes each side.
___ Mix well.
___ Put onion and garlic aside to cool.
___ Preheat frying pan and brush the burgers with oil.
___ Put all the ingredients into a bowl.
___ Fry the onion, garlic and salt until soft.

Your views

- Have you ever cooked anything? What?
- Have you ever followed a recipe?
- Do you like burgers? Does the recipe for Brilliant Beefburgers sound good?
- Would you choose to cook burgers? Which recipe would you follow?
- If you don't like burgers, what other recipe would you choose?

Working with words

A Language development
Adjectives: the past participle

1 Underline the past participle in the second sentence.

These are herbs.
They have been chopped.

- The first sentence tells you about the herbs. The second sentence tells you what has been done to them.
- These two sentences can be made into one sentence by using the past participle as an adjective.

*These are **chopped** herbs.*

2 Read these sentences. Rewrite them as one sentence. Use the past participle as an adjective.

 1 This is garlic.
   It has been crushed.

 2 This is an egg.
   It has been beaten.

- The list of ingredients for the burgers tells you what has already been done.

minced beef    **chopped** onion

3 Read this item from a list of ingredients.

4 washed carrots

What must you do with the carrots before you start cooking?

- The past participle as adjective helps to explain a recipe using fewer words so that it is quicker to read and understand.
- The past participle can describe an object or a person. It can suggest action that has already taken place without saying how it happened.

*Dad was angry about the **broken** window.*

4 Read this story beginning.

*As darkness fell, a **wounded** man crept silently out of the forest.*

What do you know has already happened?

B Making new words
Prefix *pre-*

- Some words begin *pre-*: this often means *before*.

1 Write *pre-* or *pre* in front of these words then match them to the definitions below.

____pare   ____heat   ____pay   ____dict
____view

Check in your dictionary as necessary.

1 to pay before _____
2 to say what is going to happen _____
3 to heat something before doing something else _____
4 to get something ready _____
5 to look at something before the event _____

C Spelling
Words ending *-ture*

- Some words end in *-ture*.
*You need to divide the mi**ture** into four parts.*

1 Read these definitions. Choose the correct word beginning from the box to make the word ending in *-ture*.

| sculp furni pic fu adven cul |

Use your dictionary if you aren't sure.

1 a series of exciting events: ____ture
2 the time that has not yet happened: ____ture
3 the ideas, beliefs and way of behaving of a people or nation: ____ture
4 objects in a house, like tables, chairs and cupboards: ____ture
5 an object that is carved from wood, stone or marble: ____ture
6 a drawing, painting or photograph: ____ture

Grammar

1 Read.

Sam Cooper is a young TV chef. His latest series is called *It won't bite!* Once a week, millions of viewers switch on to watch him.

"*It won't bite!* is a programme for people who are afraid of cooking," says Sam. "Basically there's nothing magic or mysterious about cooking. It's only science. **If** you **heat** water to 100° Celsius, it **boils**. **If** you **put** water in the freezer, it **becomes** ice. People understand that. It's the same with cooking. **If** you **put** a small piece of meat in the oven, it **cooks** quickly. **If** you **put** a huge chicken in the oven, it **takes** longer. If you **add** fresh herbs to your beefburgers, they **taste** better. It's obvious! People **stop** being afraid of cooking if they **understand** the science behind it. Knowledge is power! Don't you agree?"

2 Correct these sentences.
1. Sam Cooper is not very popular.
2. *It won't bite!* is his first TV series.
3. The programme is for people who love cooking.
4. If you heat water, it becomes ice.
5. If you put water in the freezer, it boils.
6. Beefburgers taste worse if you add fresh herbs.
7. People start to be afraid of cooking if they understand the science behind it.
8. If you have knowledge, you are a weaker person.

3 Find the correct endings. Write the letters.
1. Water boils ___
2. If the temperature drops to zero degrees, ___
3. Food tastes better ___
4. If you refrigerate burgers, ___
5. If burgers are thin, ___
6. Burgers take more time to cook ___
7. If you don't cook potatoes, ___
8. It is helpful to cooks ___

a if they are thick.
b if recipes are easy to follow.
c they don't fall apart when you cook them.
d water freezes.
e they take less time to cook.
f they taste horrible.
g if it is heated to 100° Celsius.
h if you use fresh ingredients.

4 Complete these sentences with words from the box.

| drink rise grow drop do use have |
| feel take produce melt freeze |

1. If temperatures ___drop___ below zero, water ___freezes___.
2. If temperatures _____ above zero, ice _____.
3. Plants _____ not _____ if they _____ not _____ sunlight.
4. We _____ energy if we _____ exercise.
5. If we _____ not _____, we _____ thirsty.
6. Our bodies _____ heat if we _____ hard physical work.

5 Think about it. Talk about it.

What happens if …
1. snow and ice become warm?
2. there is not enough rain?
3. there is too much rain?
4. a volcano erupts?

> **Remember!**
> In zero conditional sentences we use the present tense in both clauses when we are talking about general truths and scientific facts.
> If temperatures **drop** below zero, water **freezes**.
> Ice **melts** if temperatures **rise** above zero.

- Think of some more zero conditional sentences about things which are always true.

Grammar in use

Portrait Project
The shopping centre
Holly, Laura, Ross, Jack
Take photos, make a plan,
interview shoppers

1 Listen and read.

Laura: The shopping centre's very crowded today.
Ross: It's a popular place. There are always **a lot of** people here.
Holly: How can we draw a plan? It's very complicated. **Any** ideas?
Jack: There's a map on the wall over there. Can't we copy that?
Laura: I'm going to take **lots of** photos of the shops.
Jack: **Some** of the window displays are fantastic. Look at that sports shop!
Holly: The jeweller's is beautiful. There are so **many** pretty, sparkly things!
Laura: And they cost so **much** money! Don't look! You can't afford them!
Ross: We mustn't forget the café on the top floor.
Laura: How do we get up there? Is there a lift?
Holly: We can walk up the stairs or take the escalator.
Ross: I want to interview **some** shoppers and find out what they think of the shopping centre.
Jack: There are **a few** kids on that bench over there. Why don't you start with them?
Laura: I think we should split up. We've only got **a little** time.
Jack: Good thinking! Ross and I can interview **some** shoppers.
Holly: And Laura and I can go upstairs to the café.

2 Answer these questions.

1. Why are Holly, Laura, Ross and Jack at the shopping centre?
2. Are there a lot of shoppers there or only a few?
3. How many photos is Laura going to take?
4. Are all the window displays fantastic?
5. Why is the jeweller's shop window beautiful?
6. Why can't Holly afford the jewellery?
7. Are there lots of kids on the bench?
8. Why do they split up?

3 Ask and answer. Use *How much* or *How many* in the questions. Use *lots of*, *a little* or *a few* in the answers.

1. people – be – there – in the shopping centre?
   A: How many people are there in the shopping centre?
   B: There are lots of people in the shopping centre.
2. kids – be – there – on the bench?
3. photos – Laura – going to take?
4. jewellery – be – there – in the jeweller's window?
5. time – the group – have got – at the shopping centre?
6. shopping centres – be – there – in your town?
7. traffic – be – there – in the streets?
8. shops – be – there – in your street?

4 Use your own ideas to finish these sentences. Use *some* or *any*.

1. What a great sports shop! There are …
2. Look out! Don't slip! There's …
3. This café is terrible. They haven't got …
4. Here's the music shop. Have they got …?
5. This is a wonderful bakery but today there isn't …
6. Let's sit down in the café. Is there …?

Remember!

- With countable nouns use *some*, *any*, *many*, *a few*.
  There are **some** cars. There aren't **any** lorries.
  There are so **many** people! There are only **a few** children.
- With uncountable nouns use *some*, *any*, *much*, *a little*.
  There is **some** water in the jug. There isn't **any** juice.
  How **much** food have we got? We've got **a little** meat.
- Use *lots of* and *a lot of* with countable and uncountable nouns.
  There are **lots of** shops. OR There are **a lot of** shops.
  There **is lots of** time. OR There is **a lot of** time.
- We usually use *any* in questions.
  Have you got **any** money?
- We always use *any* in negative sentences.
  I haven't got **any** pets.

Grammar extra p129

Writing

Features of instructions

Instructions tell you how to do things.

▶ **Introduction**

Always begin with a clear **introduction** so the reader knows what the instructions are for:

Brilliantly Healthy Beefburgers

Try making these healthy burgers from these delicious fresh ingredients.

▶ **Layout**

Think carefully about the **layout** of the instructions.
First give a clear list of what is needed:

1 medium onion, finely chopped   a little olive oil

▶ **Order**

Then number the instructions in the correct **order**:

1 Heat the oil in a pan, add the onion, garlic and some salt and fry gently until soft.
2 Take off the heat and put aside to cool.

▶ **Short, clear sentences**

Write in **short, clear sentences** so the reader can follow the instructions easily:

Mix the ingredients well with a fork.   Repeat until they are cooked.

▶ **Use imperative verbs**

Heat the oil …

Put the mince …

ACTIVITY

Change these sentences so that they begin with an **imperative verb**.
1 It is a good idea to get all your ingredients out before you begin cooking.
2 You should chop the onion with a sharp knife.
3 I always use fresh herbs.

▶ **Use precise language**

1 tsp tomato sauce

refrigerate for **five minutes**

ACTIVITY

Say which of these phrases use **precise language** and which do not.
1 a lot of mince   2 2 garlic cloves
3 refrigerate for a bit   4 cook for three minutes
5 3 tsp chopped thyme   6 lots of tomato sauce

Writing

Writing together

> As a class you are going to rewrite some **instructions** for fish burgers so that they are clear and easy to read.

1 Read Bella's **instructions** for fish burgers. They are not very clear.

Peel some potatoes and put them in a pan to boil. You need 400 grams of them and you should add some salt to the water. Add about a 1/4 of a teaspoonful. Put a pan lid on top of a plate and put the plate on top of the pan. The fish goes on the plate and you should turn down the potatoes when they start to boil. This is a really good recipe for fish burgers. The potatoes will take 20 minutes to cook and the fish will take 15 minutes. When the fish is cooked, cut it up and mash it with some milk and the potatoes. Drain the potatoes before you mash them with the fish and milk. You need about 200 grams of fish and 2 tablespoonfuls of milk. Add some chopped parsley. Put some flour on a baking board and roll out the mixture. Form the mixture into 8 burgers and fry them. Before you fry them, coat them with egg. You need to beat the egg. Roll them in breadcrumbs. You need 2 teaspoonfuls of chopped parsley and 100 grams of breadcrumbs.

2 Sort out the **instructions**.

Make sure that they:
- begin by saying what the instructions are for
- have a clear list of ingredients
- have numbered instructions.

3 Make a neat copy of the instructions.

Individual writing **WB p63**

Listening and speaking

Conversation practice

1 Jack and Laura are talking. Look at the pictures and the words in the box. Where are Jack and Laura? What do you think they are talking about?

> some, any   a lot of, lots of
> many   much   a few   a little

2 🎧 2.03 Listen to Jack and Laura. Were you right?

3 🎧 2.03 Listen again. What do they need to buy? What do they each want to buy?

4 Talk to a friend. Imagine you are at the shopping centre or in the main shopping street in your town. Talk about what you can see in the shop windows.
Start like this:
Ooh! There are some great trainers in this window. Look at those!

Listening comprehension

1 🎧 2.04 Listen to the conversations and name the shops.

1 _____   2 _____   3 _____

2 🎧 2.04 Listen again and answer these questions.

1 In Conversation 1 who are the flowers for?
2 Why is the man buying them?
3 What colours does he buy?
4 In Conversation 2 what are they buying?
5 Why doesn't the boy like the first pair?
6 What is wrong with the second pair?
7 In Conversation 3 why will it be difficult to find what the girl wants?
8 What does she know about the book?
9 Where is it?

Individual speaking

You are going to talk about your favourite shop.   **WB p64**

A point of view   8

Check-in
People post their points of view about thousands of subjects on the internet. Other people can read what they have written and post their own views.

Have you ever read a point of view on the internet?
Have you ever commented on what someone else wrote?
Do you have a strong opinion about anything? What?
Do you enjoy hearing other people's views?

You are going to read a blog expressing a point of view about zoos.

Reading
- The writer **explains what she is writing about**, she gives her **own opinion** and she gives her **reasons**.
- She writes in the **first person**.
- She uses **persuasive language**.

Do you have a point of view about zoos?

- These words are in the blog.

 existence   stress   behaviour   instinct   cruel
captivity   boredom   isolation

What do they mean? Check in your dictionary.
What opinion do you think the writer has of zoos?

Vocabulary and spelling
- Learn words to do with **animals in captivity**.
- Learn about **negative prefixes** *in-* and *im-*.
- Learn about **homophones**, e.g. *male* and *mail*.

Think of two more pairs of homophones.

- Learn about spelling **words with *ti* / *ci* sounding *sh***.

Grammar
- Practise **first conditional**; learn **first conditional** + *unless*.
- Practise modals; learn **modals** *ought not, should not, may, might, may not, might not*.
- Practise **phrases with *get***.

Writing
- Learn about the features of writing to **express a point of view**.
- Write **a blog** giving a point of view about mobile phones.
- Write **a point of view** about homework.

Listening
- Laura, Ross and Holly's **presentation** about the design of a library for their project.
- A **discussion** between Holly and Ross about the design of buildings.
- A **speech** about plans to build houses.

Speaking
- Talk with a friend about **buildings**.
- Tell the class about **new buildings**.

Reading

Wildlife World

Member's view

This month we're posting this opinion from 16-year-old WW member, Julie Smith:

keep away from zoos - keep wildlife wild

When I was younger, I used to like going to zoos. It was really great seeing animals close up. As I have grown older, I have begun to realise precisely what sort of existence the animals have and I don't visit zoos anymore.

unnatural habitat

Animals in zoos are not free. They can't go where they like. They can't live in a natural family group. The best zoos try to give the animals the most natural habitat that they can, but a truly natural habitat is impossible. Lions born in captivity never learn to hunt. They can't use any of their natural instincts and, in my view, that is cruel.

No room to move!

animal stress

Unless you understand animal behaviour, you will not notice animal stress. When you see a tiger walking up and down, you might notice how strong and dangerous it looks. You may not know that this continual pacing, panting and pounding of paws is a sign of stress from boredom and from isolation. It is not natural behaviour. Tigers do not do this in the wild.

exploitation

Many zoos use animals to entertain visitors and to make money. If people think that it's OK to treat animals in this way, they will not try to help animals in the wild. They will think that it doesn't matter what happens to animal habitats.

action for wildlife

I'm a member of Wildlife World because I think that wild animals should be just that – wild. I tell all my friends and my brother and sisters about zoos. I explain why they shouldn't go to them. Tell your friends and family, too. Animals have a place in our lives and they ought to have a place in the world. Do people need to occupy every corner of the world? We probably could – but I'm convinced that we mustn't!

Animals need space too!

Protect natural hab

Too small, too cruel

Animals don't belong in zoos!

What do you think? Go to Members log-in. Post a response to Julie's views.

> I totally agree about the stress animals suffer when they are kept in cages. It's unbelievably cruel and shouldn't be allowed, especially not for entertainment.
> *Sam   2 hours ago*

> You're right, Julie! Well said! People must be told the real facts about zoos. Unless people get the right information, they will go on visiting them and they won't understand that these wild animals should be free.
> *Linda   4 hours ago*

> I agree that zoos should be banned. Putting animals in these prisons is a disgrace. The idea that we need zoos to learn about animals is incorrect. We can find out about animals in books, on TV and on the internet.
> *Amanda   10 hours ago*

> Zoos must be abolished! They're unkind, unfair and completely unnecessary. Get rid of them! Then let's get rid of all the circuses. Animals for entertainment? No thanks!!!
> *Jeff   1 day ago*

Wildlife World T-shirt

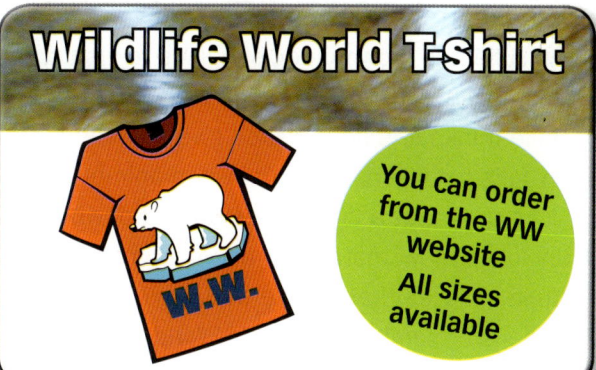

You can order from the WW website. All sizes available

WW Membership offer

Become a member of Wildlife World this month at half price!
- Receive regular email updates about WW news and events.
- Receive a log-in password to the members blog – exchange news and views.
- Get a WW T-shirt free!

Go to www.WW.gb/members

Take a wildlife holiday

Wildlife in action!
See animals in their natural habitats.

Choose from places all around the world.

Visit www.WW.gb/wildlifeholidays

Related links

Help protect sea creatures
www.nova-atlantis.org

School wildlife projects
www.wildlifeschool.com

Support wildlife in city parks
www.cityparks.com

Reading comprehension

1 Write **T (true)** *or* **F (false)**. Correct the false sentences.
1. As Julie has grown older, she likes to visit zoos to see animals close up. ____
2. Julie believes that animals in zoos are not free. ____
3. Julie thinks it is best if zoos give animals a natural habitat. ____
4. In Julie's opinion, it is cruel when animals cannot use their natural instincts. ____
5. Julie says that a tiger paces up and down because it is strong and dangerous. ____
6. In Julie's view, many zoos use animals to entertain visitors and to make money. ____
7. Julie believes that people who exploit animals in zoos will not help animals in the wild. ____
8. Julie is a member of Wildlife World so she can tell her friends about it. ____
9. Julie tells her friends and family to visit animals in zoos. ____
10. Julie believes that people need to occupy every corner of the world. ____

2 Discuss these questions about the web page.
1. Who do you think the whole web page is for?
2. How can members post a response to Julie's blog?
3. Do you think many members have read Julie's views? Why? / Why not?
4. What sort of activities does Wildlife World try to interest people in?
5. Which section of the web page has similar websites about nature?

3 Match these nouns from the web page to the correct definition.

| exploitation captivity isolation instincts boredom behaviour existence |

1. the feeling of having nothing interesting to do _____
2. way of living _____
3. separation from other people or things _____
4. the use of something or somebody in an unfair way to get something for yourself _____
5. a situation of being not free _____
6. what a person or animal does _____
7. feelings and needs that are natural to a person or animal _____

What kind of nouns are they?

4 Scan the text and find the words. Discuss the answers to the questions.
1. Find three actions by the tiger that are signs of stress. _____ _____ _____
   What letter do they begin with?
2. Find three adjectives describing zoos that begin with the same negative prefix *un-*.
   _____ _____ _____
   Why do you think the writer has chosen words with the same beginning?

5 Talk about the answers to these questions.
1. If you were Julie, what would you think about the responses sent in by other members? Why?
2. Are there any new, different ideas in the responses?
3. What are they?
4. Do you agree or disagree with Julie?
5. Do you agree or disagree with any of the responses?

Your views
- Is it useful for people to post their opinions on a website?
- What is good about blogging? Is there anything bad about it?
- Do you have a strong opinion about anything that you would like to tell other people about?

Working with words

A Making new words
More about prefixes

- A prefix changes the meaning of a word.
  do to carry out an action
  redo to carry out the action again

Negative prefixes
- A negative prefix makes a word change its meaning to the opposite meaning. You already know these negative prefixes:
  un- **un**usual   dis- **dis**agree
- im- and in- are two more negative prefixes:
  impossible … a truly natural habitat is **im**possible.
  incorrect The idea that we need zoos to learn about animals is **in**correct.
- If the affirmative word begins with *p*, the negative prefix is usually *im-*.

1 Read these words that use the negative prefixes *im-* and *in-*. Write the affirmative word next to each negative.

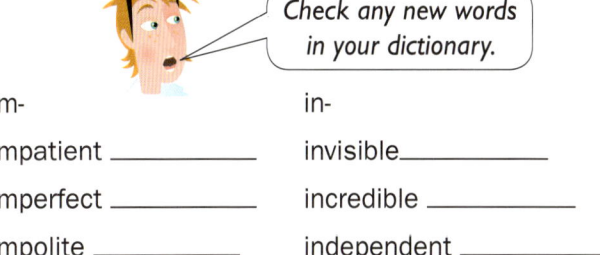
Check any new words in your dictionary.

im-	in-
impatient _____	invisible _____
imperfect _____	incredible _____
impolite _____	independent _____

2 Write the correct negative prefix *in-* or *im-* in front of these words.

_____possible   _____direct   _____formal
_____probable   _____separable

3 Don't get confused! Read these words and their opposites.

important – **un**important
interested – **un**interested

im- or in- at the start of a word is not always a negative prefix.

B Spelling
Homophones

- Some words sound the same but they are spelled differently. These words are called **homophones**.

1 Look at the spelling of these pairs of words. Read each pair. The words sound the same.

1	sauce	source
2	roll	role
3	allowed	aloud
4	floe	flow
5	male	mail
6	shore	sure

You have already read the words in the left column in this book!

Check any new words in the column on the right in your dictionary.

Words with *ci* / *ti*

- Some words have *ci* or *ti* that make the sound *sh*.
  espe**ci**ally It shouldn't be allowed, espe**ci**ally not for entertainment.
  ac**ti**on   Wildlife in ac**ti**on!

2 Read and say these words.

Check you understand them.

optician

ancient

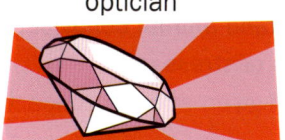
precious

patient

delicious

initial

official

cautious

Working with words: negative prefixes; homophones; words with *ci* / *ti*

Grammar

1 **Read.**

You **will see** many different animals **if** you **visit** a zoo. **If** it **is** a good zoo, the animals **will have** plenty of space. **If** it **is** a bad zoo, the animals **will** probably **be** in small enclosures.

Some people believe that all zoos are bad and that **if** a wild animal **is held** in captivity, it **will suffer** from stress. It is true that **if** a tiger **is kept** in a small cage, it **will pace** up and down. **If** a lion **is born** in captivity, **it will** never **learn** to hunt. It will not have the chance to use its natural instincts.

Unless people **are given** the correct information about zoos, they **will go on** visiting them. **Unless** they **are** aware of animal cruelty, they **will** not **understand** that wild animals should be free.

2 Find the correct endings. Write the letters.

1. If a zoo is good, ___
2. If a zoo is bad, ___
3. A tiger will pace up and down ___
4. Wild animals will suffer from stress ___
5. A lion will not learn to hunt ___
6. If a lion is born in captivity, ___

a if it suffers from stress.
b it will not have the chance to use its natural instincts.
c animals will not be held in small cages.
d if it is born in captivity.
e animals will not have plenty of space.
f if they are held in captivity.

3 Change the sentences. Use *unless*. Make sure the sentences have the same meaning.

1. If people do not understand animal behaviour, they will not spot the signs of stress.
   Unless people understand animal behaviour, they will not spot the signs of stress.
2. If a wild animal is not given enough space, it will suffer from stress.
3. A lion will not learn to hunt if it is not born in the wild.
4. People will not understand animal behaviour if they are not taught about it.
5. If people are not given the correct information, they will go on visiting zoos.
6. Animal cruelty will continue if we do not protest about it.

4 Complete these sentences with the verbs in brackets.

1. If you ___*visit*___ the zoo, you ___*will see*___ fascinating animals. (visit, see)
2. If a wild animal _____ in a cage, it _____ soon _____ depressed. (live, become)
3. Lions _____ never _____ to hunt if they _____ born in captivity. (learn, be)
4. Unless people _____ hunting rhino, they _____ from the African plains. (stop, disappear)
5. Polar bears _____ unless we _____ their environment. (die out, protect)

5 Use your own ideas to finish these sentences.

1. Unless we protect animals like pandas, …
2. Animals in zoos will continue to feel stressed unless …
3. Rare animals will die out if …

> **Remember!**
> In first conditional sentences we are thinking about the future. Use the future tense in the main clause. Use the present tense in the *if* clause.
> We **will go** to the beach **if** the weather **is** fine.
> **If** you **go** to France, you **will learn** French.
> **Unless** means *if not*.
> **If** Joe **doesn't work** harder, he **will fail** his exams.
> **Unless** Joe **works** harder, he **will fail** his exams.
> I **won't go** to the party **if** you **don't go** with me.
> I **won't go** to the party **unless** you **go** with me.

- **Think of some more first conditional sentences using *if* and *unless*.**

Grammar in use

Portrait Project
New buildings: plans for the new library Ross, Holly and Laura at the proposed site Video

1 🎧 2.06 **Listen and read.**

Laura: Are you ready? Have you got the picture, Holly? OK … Off you go!
Ross: Today we're at Greenfields Park in the centre of town.
Holly: As you **can see**, it's a vast green space but soon it **may look** very different.
Ross: Yes, in six months' time this beautiful park **may be lost** forever.
Holly: It **might become** a noisy, dirty building site.
Ross: This is where the council wants to build our new town library.
Holly: And what a library it is!
Laura: You **must hold up** the picture, Holly!
Holly: Oh, yes! Sorry!
Ross: The library will be built mainly of glass and steel.
Holly: We certainly need a new library but not everyone in the town is happy with this location or the proposed design.
Ross: Some people feel that such a modern building **should not be built** next to the traditional stone buildings in the centre of town.
Holly: Others say that we **ought not to build** on the precious open spaces in our town.
Ross: So will Hampton get its new library? It **might** …
Holly: Or it **might not** …
Laura: Great! That was brilliant! Well done!

2 Answer these questions.
1. Where is Greenfields Park? What is it like?
2. What might happen to the park?
3. What does the council want to build there?
4. Is the design modern or traditional?
5. Is everyone happy with the design?
6. Will Hampton get its new library?

3 Ask and answer. Use *may* or *might*.
1. Hampton – get – a new library? (might)
   A: Will Hampton get a new library?
   B: It might get a new library but it might not.
2. Greenfields Park – disappear? (might)
3. the town's open spaces – be destroyed? (may)
4. everyone – like – the design? (might)
5. the plans – be changed? (may)
6. the library – be built? (might)

4 Read and make sentences. Use the verbs in brackets.
1. Your friend has difficulty reading the words on the blackboard. What advice do you give him? (shouldn't / ought to)
2. Your friend is worried because he failed his last science test. What advice do you give him? (ought not to / should)
3. You didn't finish your homework. What excuse do you give to your teacher? (couldn't)
4. You didn't hear what your friend said. What do you ask him? (can)
5. Someone is bullying your friend. What advice do give your friend? (mustn't / must)

Remember!
Modal verbs: *may, might, can, could, should, ought to, must*
- Affirmative: subject + modal verb + infinitive without *to* (except *ought to*)
  It **might rain**. You **ought to leave**.
- Interrogative: modal verb + subject + infinitive without *to* (except *ought to*)
  Must we **take** a test? **Ought** you **to do** that?
- Negative: subject + modal verb + *not* + infinitive without *to* (except *ought to*)
  She **could not swim**. He **ought not to shout**.
- Passive: subject + modal verb + passive infinitive without *to* (except *ought to*)
  A bridge **should be built**. The questions **must be answered**. That tree **ought to be cut down**.

• Think of some more sentences with *may, might, can, could, should, ought to* and *must*.

Grammar extra p129

Writing

Features of expressing a point of view

> When you **express a point of view**, it is important that you make clear:
> - what you are writing about
> - what your opinion is

▶ **First paragraph**

Make it clear in the **first paragraph** what you are writing about. In the web page on page 78 Julie Smith begins by saying that she used to visit zoos but:

> … I have begun to realise precisely what sort of existence the animals have and I don't visit zoos anymore.

▶ **Reasons**

Follow your opening paragraph with **reasons** that support your opinion. Julie's reasons for disliking zoos are that the animals:
- do not live in their natural habitat
- suffer stress
- are exploited.

She uses a paragraph to explain each reason.

▶ **First person**

You are expressing your opinion so write in the **first person**.

> … **I** don't visit zoos anymore.

> **I'm** a member of Wildlife World …

ACTIVITY

Change these third person sentences into **first person sentences**.
1. He was upset when he saw the animals in the cages. He went home very unhappy.
2. He told his friends they shouldn't visit zoos anymore.

▶ **Second person**

A writer will often use the **second person** to get the reader involved.

> … **you** will not notice animal stress.

> Tell **your** friends and family, too.

▶ **Persuasive language**

When you express an opinion, you often want people to agree with you. The **words** you choose can be very **persuasive**.

ACTIVITY

1. … making 'a truly natural habitat is **impossible**'. Is this more persuasive than 'difficult'? Why?
2. Animals 'can't use their natural instincts and, in my view, that is **cruel**'. Is this more persuasive than 'not nice'? Why?
3. The tiger is under so much stress that we see a 'continual **pacing, panting and pounding of paws**'. Is this more persuasive than 'the tiger walks up and down a lot'? Why?

Writing

Writing together

> Mobile phones are part of our everyday life. Some people can't think how they managed without them! Some people hate them!
> As a class you are going to write your **opinion** of mobile phones.

1 **Discuss** mobile phones.
- How many students in the class have one?
- How many students don't?

2 Make a **list** of advantages and disadvantages of mobile phones.

> Advantages
> You do not need to be near a public phone.

> Disadvantages
> They are expensive.

3 Take a **vote**.
- How many students think mobile phones are a good invention?
- How many students think mobile phones are a bad invention?

4 Write a **blog** expressing the opinion that:

> Mobile phones are a good invention.
> OR
> Mobile phones are a bad invention.

Here are some **persuasive** words and phrases you could use:

  fantastic   easy to use   never 'alone' with a mobile phone
     quick   efficient   noisy   expensive   annoying

Remember!
- Use your first paragraph to introduce the subject of mobile phones.
- Use a new paragraph for each reason you use to support your opinion.
- Use the first person (*I / we*) to express your opinion.
- Use the second person (*you*) to get the reader involved.
- Use language to persuade the reader to agree with you.

Individual writing WB p71

Listening and speaking

Conversation practice

1 Holly and Ross are talking. Look at the pictures and the words in the box. What do you think they are talking about?

> should   shouldn't   ought to   ought not to   might   might not
> storeys   views   modern   traditional   skyscraper   palace

2 🎧 2.07 Listen to Holly and Ross. Were you right?

3 🎧 2.07 Read the phrases in the box. Then listen again and spot the phrases.

> I'm not sure.   your kind of thing   This is more like it.   You've got to be joking.
> deadly serious   I expect   What's the matter?   Exactly!

4 Talk to a friend about the pictures above. Talk about the kind of buildings that you like. Use some of the phrases in the box if you can. Start like this:

Look at that skyscraper! It's so high!

Listening comprehension

1 🎧 2.08 Listen to Maggie James. Circle the right answers.
  1 What is her job?   **architect / teacher / environmentalist / vet**
  2 Where is she speaking?   **at a meeting / on the phone / on the radio**

2 🎧 2.08 Listen again. Underline the mistakes.
  1 The council is planning to build a few new homes.
  2 The town doesn't need more houses.
  3 The proposed site is Four Oaks Park.
  4 Many rare plants grow in the river.
  5 An unusual type of frog lives in the river.
  6 The woods are not very old.
  7 The woods are a dangerous habitat for many creatures.
  8 Maggie James wants the townspeople to agree with the council.

Correct the sentences.

Individual speaking

You are going to talk about new buildings in your town or city.   **WB p72**

How the body works

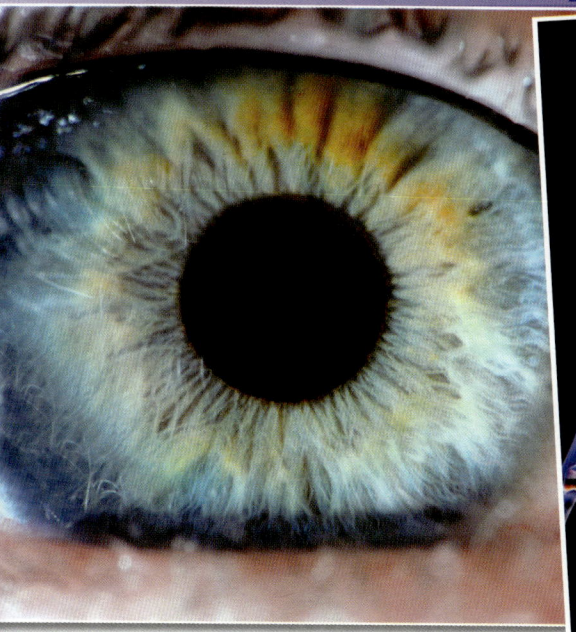
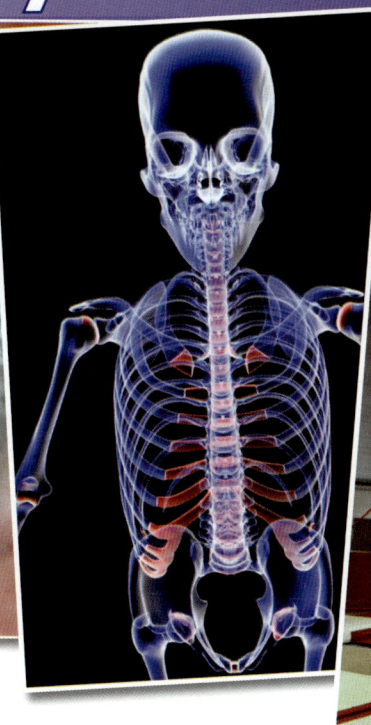

9

Check-in

Different parts of our bodies work in particular ways. We understand how many of them work.

When you breathe in, where does the air go to?
What pushes blood around your body?
Which part of your body do sound waves pass into?
Which part of your body does light pass through?

You are going to read an explanation of how your eyes work.

Reading

- The **explanation** is written in the **order** that things happen.
- It is written in the **present tense** and uses the **present simple** and the **present simple passive**.
- The explanation includes **diagrams**.

Why is a diagram useful in an explanation?

- These words are in the explanation.

   brain   approximately   muscle   transparent
   human   automatically   weld

What do they mean? Check in your dictionary.

Vocabulary and spelling

- Learn words to do with the **eye** and **sight**.
- Learn words with **suffixes -ible** and **-able**.
- Learn about **gerunds**: *I like swimming*.
- Learn about spelling **words ending -sion**.

Grammar

- Practise **passives**: present, past, future, present perfect.
- Practise **question tags** with *is / do*: *It's big, isn't it?*
- Learn **question tags with negative statements**: *It isn't big, is it?*
- Practise **phrases with** *shut*.

Writing

- Learn about **features of writing an explanation**.
- **Write an explanation** of how we breathe.
- **Write an explanation** of how your arms move.

Listening

- Laura and Ross **discussing** things in a market.
- Holly and Laura **discussing** pictures of market stalls.
- An **interview** with a market stallholder.

Is there a street market near your home? What can you buy there?

Speaking

- Talk with a friend about **a market**.
- Tell the class about a **market in your town** or one you have visited.

87

Reading

How we see

An eye is like a living camera. It detects light from surrounding objects. It focuses the light to a picture which is understood by the brain. The picture that travels to the back of your eye is upside-down. Your brain turns it the right way up.

the object / what your eye sees / the final image

How the eye works

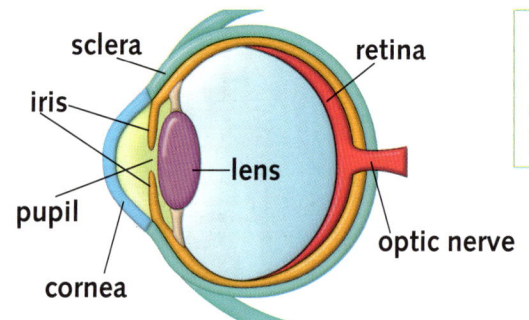

The diagram shows a human eye. The human eye is approximately 2.54cm wide, 2.54cm deep and 2.3cm tall. Each part of the eye has a different purpose.

First, light passes into your eye through the pupil. In bright light it is smaller because less light is needed to see objects. It becomes bigger in dull light so that more light enters the eye and helps you to see objects more clearly.

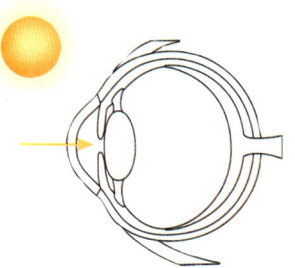 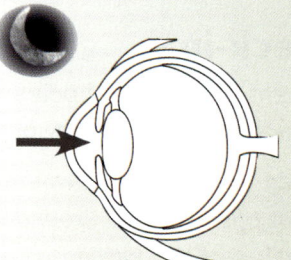

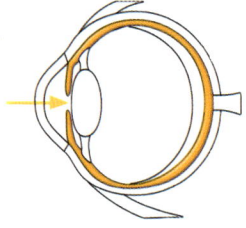 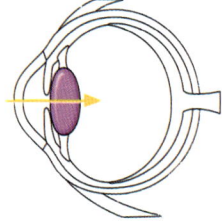 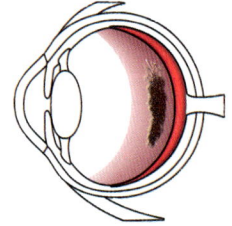 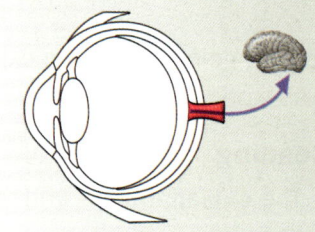

The iris controls the amount of light that enters the eye. Muscles in the iris make the pupil larger or smaller. The iris is the coloured part of your eye.

Next, the light passes through the lens. The lens focuses light onto the retina. The lens changes shape to make sure that the picture on the retina is as clear as possible.

The retina acts like a movie screen and shows the picture you are seeing – upside-down. It turns the picture into an electrical message for the brain.

Finally, the optic nerve sends electrical messages from the retina to the brain. The brain turns the image the right way up.

The eye's built-in protection

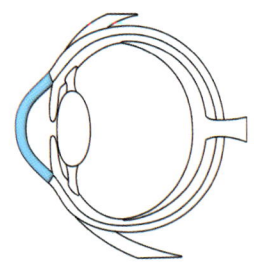

The cornea is the transparent skin that covers the front of your eye and protects it. In particular, it protects the iris.

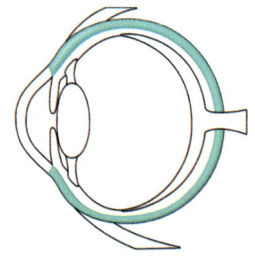

The outside of the eyeball is protected by the sclera. It is made of tough skin that covers all parts of the eye except the cornea. It supports and protects the eye.

Our amazing eyes

Humans have binocular vision. That means that both eyes work together. They are placed at the front of our heads and we are good at telling how far away something is and how fast it is moving. In the past, our vision helped us to hunt in order to survive. We no longer hunt in the same way but we use our vision to help us in many different ways in our daily lives. With your eyes you can see an object as small as 0.1mm across. You can tell the difference between 10 million different shades of colour. It seems impossible, doesn't it? Our eyes are important and they need protection from damage and injury.

Natural eye care
Your eyelids and eyelashes protect your eyes. Eyelids can partly close and act as sunshades in bright light. They can shut out light completely when you sleep. They can close automatically if something is flying towards your eye. Your eyelashes trap dust that flies into your eye.

Tears wash your eyes. There are tear glands inside the upper eye lid. Tears form all the time and blinking spreads the tears across your eye to help keep them clean and comfortable.

Extra eye protection

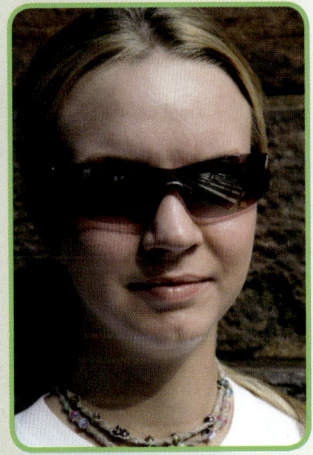
Very bright light can harm your eyes. This girl is wearing sunglasses. When she goes into bright sunlight, her eyes will be protected by the dark lenses.

Small pieces of hot or sharp material can injure your eyes. This man is working with hot metal. When he welded two pieces together, the sparks began to fly. His eyes were protected by the thick plastic in the visor of his helmet.

Goggles have been worn by motorcyclists for more than 100 years. They give protection from the wind, from insects and from dust.

Baseball catchers wear batting helmets with a metal visor to protect their eyes from the ball. It's not surprising, is it? In a baseball game, the ball can travel at up to 160kph. Ouch!

Reading: an explanation

Reading comprehension

1 **Answer these questions.**
1. What does the eye detect from surrounding objects?
2. Which way up is the picture that travels to the back of your eye?
3. What turns it the right way up?
4. What is the pupil at the front of your eye?
5. What does the iris do?
6. What part of the eye protects the iris?
7. What is the sclera made of and what does it do?
8. What does the lens do?
9. How does the retina work?
10. How do electrical messages travel from the retina to the brain?

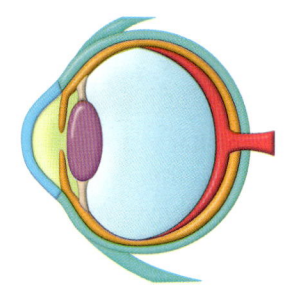

2 **Choose the correct word or phrase to complete the sentences.**
1. Humans have binocular **views / eyes / vision**.
2. In the past, our vision helped us to hunt in order to **survive / eat / kill**.
3. With your eyes, you can see an object as small as **0.01mm / 0.1mm / 1.0mm** across.
4. Eyelids can partly close and act as **sunglasses / sunshades / sunhats**.
5. Your eyelashes trap **flies / tears / dust**.
6. Tears wash your **eyes / eyelids / cheeks**.
7. Tears are spread across your eye when you **cry / blink / sleep**.

3 **Discuss your answers to these questions.**
1. Which parts of the eye did you already know about?
2. Which facts about the eye do you think are the most surprising?
3. Which things give natural protection and care to your eyes? What protection do they give?
4. How many different dangers do the eyes need to be protected from? Write a list.

4 **Match the different kinds of eye protection.**

1. sunglasses 2. plastic visor 3. metal visor 4. goggles

a

b
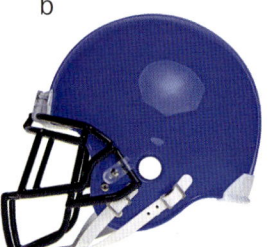

c

d

Your views
- Which of the kinds of eye protection do you have?
- Have you ever used any of the others?
- Do you think you might need eye protection in the future?
- What sort of activities do you think you might need it for?

Working with words

A Making new words

Adjectives ending -ible

> Some adjectives end in -ible.
> You can tell the difference between 10 million shades of colour. It seems imposs**ible**, doesn't it?

1 Complete these adjectives ending in -ible then answer the questions.

terr_____   vis_____   horr_____

cred_____   sens_____   divis_____

1 Which two words mean 'very bad'? _____
2 Which word means 'wise, having reason'? _____
3 Which word means 'can be seen'? _____
4 Which word means 'can be split up into smaller parts'? _____
5 Which word means 'can be believed'? _____

Adjectives ending -able

> Some verbs can be made into adjectives by adding -able.
> Blinking spreads tears across your eyes to help keep them clean and comfort**able**.

2 Read these adjectives. Write the verb.

1 breakable _____
2 believable _____
3 lovable _____
4 separable _____

Look in your dictionary if you aren't sure.

3 Look at these words.

lovable   believable

What do you think the rule for adding the suffix -able is? Write the rule.

_____
_____

Look out! *These words don't follow the rule.*

lik**e**able   notic**e**able

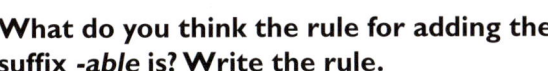

4 Find words in Activities 1 and 2 that mean the same, or nearly the same, as these words.

believable _____   likeable _____
divisible _____   terrible _____

B Gerunds

> Verbs ending -ing can be used as nouns. They are called **gerunds**.
> You have practised verb + **gerund**.
> I like **swimming**. I don't mind **running** but I prefer **playing** basketball.

1 Read these pairs of sentences. The second sentence in each pair begins with a gerund. Underline the gerund.

1 This man is welding. Welding is dangerous work.
2 This girl is on skis. Skiing is an Olympic sport.

2 Complete these sentences with the correct gerund.

1 Motorbike riders wear goggles. _____ goggles protects their eyes.
2 This baseball player is wearing a visor. _____ baseball can be dangerous.

C Spelling

Words ending -sion

> Some words end in -sion. The ending sounds /ʒən/.

1 Read these words. Tick the words you know. Look up any new words in your dictionary.

explosion ☐   vision ☐   television ☐
revision ☐   decision ☐   confusion ☐
inclusion ☐

Remember, some words end -ssion.

2 Read these words. How does the ending sound?

session
mission
discussion
impression

Don't get confused!

Grammar

1 **Read.**

Light passes into your eye through the pupil. The amount of light that enters your eye **is controlled** by the iris, the coloured part of the eye. The picture of what you are seeing appears on the retina at the back of the eye. This picture **is turned** into an electrical message by the retina. The message **is sent** from the retina to the brain by the optic nerve.

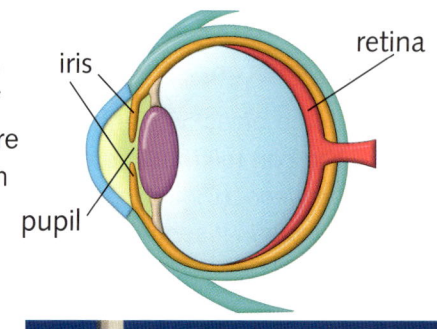

This girl is wearing sunglasses. Her eyes **will be protected** when she goes outside into bright sunlight.

In sport, helmets and goggles **have been worn** for many years to protect the eyes of sportsmen and sportswomen.

The first snow goggles **were worn** by the Inuit people two thousand years ago. They **were made** of ivory.

2 Cover the text. Read the sentences below and write T (true) or F (false).

1 The coloured part of the eye is called the retina. ___
2 A picture appears on the retina. ___
3 An electrical message is sent to the brain by the retina. ___
4 Sportsmen have worn helmets and goggles for a few years. ___
5 The first snow goggles were worn by the Inuit people. ___
6 They were made of glass. ___

Compare your answers. Uncover the text and check. Correct the false sentences.

3 Change these sentences. Use the passive.

1 Someone has broken the window.
   The window has been broken.
2 Someone has stolen my camera.
3 People clean the streets every day.
4 Someone will announce the results tomorrow.
5 Someone damaged Ben's bike.
6 They took the photographs in the evening.

4 Ask and answer. Use the passive in your answers.

1 What covers the front of the eye? (the cornea)
   The front of the eye is covered by the cornea.
2 What sends messages to the brain? (the optic nerve)
3 Who will take the exam? (the whole school)
4 Who has won the first prize? (a student from Moscow)
5 What has blown down the trees? (strong winds)

5 Use the passive. Answer these questions.

1 Who wrote your favourite book?
2 When was your school built?
3 Who teaches English in your school?
4 What sports are played at your school?

Talk about your answers.

> **Remember!**
> We use the passive when:
> - we do not know who does the action
> - we do not care who does the action
> - we know who does the action but we do not want to say.
>   *Dad's car **was stolen**.*
>   *The painting **will be sold**.*
>   *A window **has been broken**.*
> We also use the passive when the person or thing that does the action is important or significant.
> *The town **has been damaged** by a violent storm.*
> The passive = to be + past participle.

- Think of some more sentences using the passive.

Grammar in use

Portrait Project
Street market
Ross and Laura
Photos and interviews

1 🎧 Listen and read.

Laura: Here we are! Goose Lane market!
Ross: The market isn't here every day, **is it**?
Laura: No, just once a week, on Thursdays.
Ross: It's very busy, **isn't it**?
Laura: Yes, it's really popular. Loads of people come here.
Ross: But the prices are rather high, **aren't they**?
Laura: You don't go shopping very often, **do you**? Everything's much cheaper here than at the supermarket.
Ross: There are so many stalls! Fruit and vegetables, clothes, textiles, crockery, cutlery, pots and pans … They sell everything here, **don't they**?
Laura: Almost everything! We'll get some good photos. It's really colourful.
Ross: Take a photo of that fish stall. It's amazing!
Laura: And that cheese looks good, too, **doesn't it**?
Ross: I'm going to interview some stallholders.
Laura: Right. What about that woman over there?
Ross: She doesn't look too busy, **does she**? What's she selling in those jars?
Laura: The sign on the stall says 'Home-made honey'.
Ross: I love honey! And I can talk to her about keeping bees.
Laura: Yes, that's really interesting.
Ross: And maybe she'll give me a free sample!
Laura: Ross! You're so greedy!

2 Answer these questions.
1. Is the market open every day?
2. Do people like the market?
3. What food is sold at the market? Name five things.
4. Why is it a good place to take photos?
5. Who is Ross going to interview?
6. What does he hope he will get?

3 Read these sentences aloud and add a question tag.

Remember!
When the sentence is negative, the question tag is affirmative: *The shops **aren't** open, **are they**?*

1. The market isn't expensive.
   The market isn't expensive, is it?
2. The stallholders don't sell everything.
3. The lady selling honey doesn't look busy.
4. The textiles aren't expensive.
5. You don't go shopping very often.
6. Ross isn't taking photos.
7. You aren't interested in shopping.
8. The market doesn't open on Tuesdays.

4 Add question tags to these sentences.

Remember!
When the sentence is affirmative, the question tag is negative: *The lady is **selling** honey, **isn't she**?*

1. Ross loves honey.
   Ross loves honey, doesn't he?
2. The fish on that stall looks fresh.
3. Laura is good at photography.
4. The stalls look very colourful.
5. That lady makes her own honey.
6. The prices are quite low.
7. You often shop at the market.
8. Ross is very greedy.

Grammar extra p129

Writing

Features of explanations

> You have read an **explanation** about how the eye works.
> **Explanations** tell us how or why something happens.

▶ **First paragraph**

It is made clear in the **first paragraph** what is being **explained**.

> An eye is like a living camera. It detects light from surrounding objects. It focuses the light to a picture which is understood by the brain.

▶ **Present tenses**

Explanations are usually written in **present tenses**.

Present simple

light passes

becomes bigger

Present simple passive

is protected

is made of

Copy and complete the chart.

Verb	Present simple	Present simple passive
1 pass	It _____	It _____
2 turn	It _____	It _____
3 control	It _____	It _____
4 cover	It _____	It _____
5 protect	It _____	It _____
6 focus	It _____	It _____

▶ **Sequence**

Explanations are written in the **order** that things happen.

> **First,** light passes into your eye through the pupil.

> **Next,** the light passes through the lens.

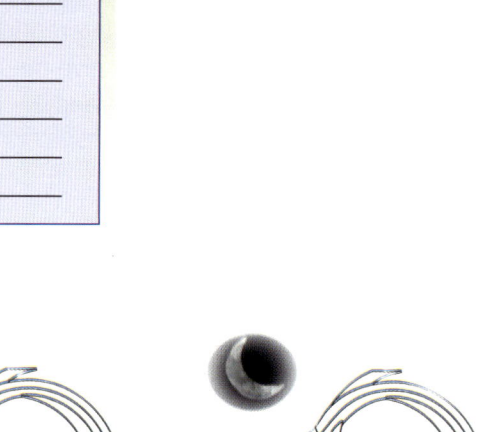

▶ **Cause and effect**

In explanations, 'something' causes 'something else' to happen. **Linking words and phrases** help to show this.

> It becomes bigger in dull light **so that** more light enters the eye.

> The lens changes shape **to make sure that** the picture on the retina is as clear as possible.

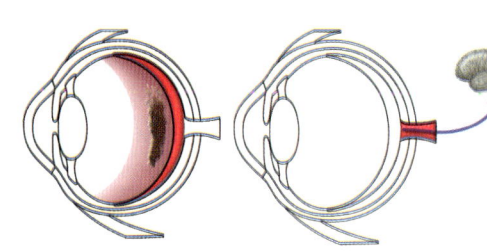

▶ **Illustrations**

Explanations often have **diagrams** to help the reader 'see' the stages of what is being explained.

Writing

Writing together

> You have read an **explanation** of how the eye works.
> As a class you are going to **explain** how air gets into our lungs.

1 Discuss what you know about how we breathe.

2 This is an explanation of how air gets into our lungs but it is incomplete. Complete the explanation.
- Use the labels in each diagram to complete the sentences.
- Put the verbs in brackets into the present tense.

1 nose, nasal cavity, mouth

1 We _____ (breathe) air through the _____ and into the _____ _____.
We also _____ (take) in air through the _____.

2 pharynx, larynx

2 The air _____ (pass) through the _____ and into the _____.

3 trachea

3 The larynx is _____ (connect) to the _____. The air _____ (move) from the larynx through to the trachea.

4 bronchi, right lung, left lung

4 The trachea _____ (branch) into two _____. One _____ (go) to the _____ _____ and the other to the _____ _____.

5 bronchioles

5 Each of the two _____ is _____ (divide) into about 20 _____.

6 sacs, alveoli

6 The _____ _____ (end) in tiny _____. These are _____ (make) of small _____. This is where oxygen from the air is _____ (absorb) into the blood.

Individual writing

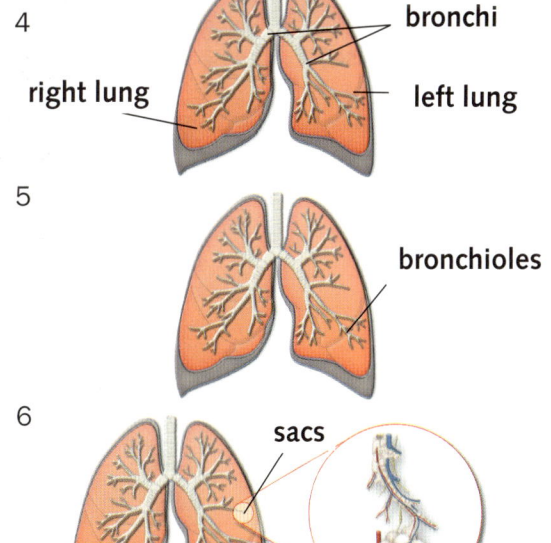

WB p81

Writing together: an explanation **95**

Listening and speaking

Conversation practice

1 Holly and Laura are talking. Look at the pictures and the words in the box. What do you think they are talking about?

| buy   sell   wear   colourful   beautiful   amazing   fantastic   is it?   isn't it? |
| are they?   aren't they?   does it?   doesn't it?   do they?   don't they? |

2 Listen to Holly and Laura. Were you right?

3 Read the phrases in the box. Then listen again and spot the phrases.

| loads of stuff   Thanks a lot.   Gosh!   Don't be mean!   No, not at all! |
| Actually …   I suppose so.   Absolutely! |

4 Talk to a friend about a market in your town. Talk about the different stalls and what you can buy there. Use some of the phrases in the box if you can. Start like this:

Have you ever been to the market, (name)? What can you buy there?

Listening comprehension

1 Laura is interviewing a young man at the market. Listen and answer these questions.

 1 Does Jamie live in the town or in the country?   2 What is he doing at the market?
 3 Is he happy with his life?

2 Read these sentences. Then listen again and write T (true) or F (false).

 1 Jamie comes to the market twice a week. ___
 2 He is selling cheese from his family's farm. ___
 3 The cheese is not made in a traditional way. ___
 4 Complicated machinery is needed to make the cheese. ___
 5 His family has been making cheese for many years. ___
 6 Jamie wants to stay on the farm and carry on the tradition. ___
 7 Jamie wants to see the world. ___
 8 He has discussed his plans with his father. ___

 Correct the false sentences.

3 Talk about it. What do you think Jamie should do?

Individual speaking

You are going to talk about a market in your town or a market you have visited.

WB p82

Later that day ... 10

Check-in
An interesting story has a good plot.
The plot is the main events in the story, how and why they happen.

Write the title of a book or film that has a good plot.
Write down two main events in the plot.
Write down three adjectives to describe the plot.

You are going to read a narrative story of several events.

Reading
- The story is written in the **past tense**.
- It has a **beginning**, a **middle** and an **end**.
- The events are told in the **order** that they happen.
- It includes some **direct speech**.

What punctuation do you need for direct speech?

- These words are in the story.
  lonely   depressed   cheerfulness   radiant   certainty
          inspire   embarrass   modestly

What do they mean? Check in your dictionary.

Vocabulary and spelling
- Learn words to do with **behaviour** and **feelings**.
- Learn about **adjectival phrases** and the **suffix -ous**.
- Learn about spelling **words ending -er** and **-re**.

Grammar
- Practise the **present perfect simple** and **continuous** with *for / since*.
- Practise the **present perfect** with *ever / never* and the **past tense**.
- Practise **phrases with** *go*.

Writing
- Learn about the **features of story plots**.
- Write a **narrative story** with a beginning, a middle and an end.
- Write a **story** from a given plot and pictures.

Listening
- Jack, Laura and Ross's **conversation** about a Town Fair.
- Holly and Jack's **discussion** about pictures of international festivals.
- A **dialogue** about traditional English dancing.

Speaking
- Talk with a friend about **international festivals**.
- Tell the class about **a festival you know about**.

Reading

A helping hand

"Tremendous news!" Mum sighed with relief as she put down the phone. "Grandma's operation was successful but she has to stay in hospital to rest for a while. I'll go and see her tomorrow."

When Mum came back the next evening, she looked concerned. "Isn't Grandma all right?" asked Sadie, glancing up from her chemistry text book.

"She feels lonely," Mum said. "She misses us and she doesn't know what we're all doing."

"Didn't you tell her that I've been revising hard for my exams since she went into hospital?" asked Sadie. "Did you tell her my teacher has chosen my report on the Centre for Biological Sciences for the school magazine?"

Annette didn't say anything. She had no news that Mum could tell Grandma.

"Yes, I did," said Mum, "but she seems really depressed. She says she's no use to anyone anymore."

At lunch the next day, everyone suggested ideas to cheer Grandma up.

Sadie said, "I could take her to the university and show her where I'll be studying next year."

Dad said, "Grandma's favourite opera is at the theatre next month. I'll get tickets."

Mum said, "I'll make new curtains for Grandma's bedroom. She hasn't had new curtains for years."

Annette wished she had something exciting for Grandma but she needed to concentrate on her photography project for her art exam and she didn't have time to think of anything else.

Over the next few weeks, Annette kept her camera with her all the time, ready for every opportunity. She was ready when Sadie got her exam results in a crisp, white envelope early one morning and ready again half an hour later when Sadie's friends came round and they stood next to Mum's little lemon tree on the balcony, crying, laughing and hugging each other. She had her camera when Mum was choosing curtain material at the stall in the market. She had it on a number of other occasions, too. Eventually, she had plenty of pictures for her project and she knew what to do for Grandma.

Four weeks later, Grandma was pleased to see the medical faculty at the university where Sadie would be starting in a few weeks. She enjoyed her visit to the opera and she thanked Mum for the new curtains in her bedroom but she had not regained her usual cheerfulness. One afternoon, Annette gave her an album of photographs. Grandma spent a long time looking at the pictures: Sadie's radiant face above a large sheet of white paper, Sadie and her friends beaming in front of the lemon tree, Mum leaning over the material stall surrounded by a rainbow of translucent silks and satins, shimmering gently in the breeze.

"Have you ever realised, Annette," said Grandma, "what a marvellous talent you have?"

Annette sighed. "I've never been good at exams, like Sadie. I got terrible marks last year. I probably won't get a good grade this year and anyway, art isn't an important subject."

"Isn't it? Isn't it important to notice things that are beautiful and interesting?" enquired Grandma.

"It's not as important as being able to make people well, like a doctor," Annette answered with certainty.

"Doctors can make your body better, but it takes more than a doctor to inspire people with beauty and to make them think, Annette. Not everyone can do what you can do." Grandma paused for a moment then she said, "There's a photography competition at the art gallery. Why don't you enter one of your pictures?"

Annette just laughed and shook her head but she went on thinking about Grandma's suggestion. Was her work good enough? She didn't know. She wasn't sure that Grandma knew, either. She didn't want to be embarrassed. She went on thinking all the same.

A month later, it was Annette who got an envelope early one morning. Inside was a letter and a cheque. Everyone looked at Annette enquiringly.

"I entered a photography competition. I didn't win. I got third prize," said Annette, modestly.

Everyone was pleased and impressed.

Later that day, Annette told her grandmother that she had decided to study photography next year. Ultimately, she would like to go to art college.

"Have you made that decision since you got the prize?" asked Grandma.

"No, I've been thinking about it for weeks – since we last talked, in fact. You gave me confidence."

"I'm glad you found our chat useful," said Grandma cheerfully.

Mum, listening from the doorway, breathed another sigh of relief.

Reading comprehension

1 **Read the sentences carefully. Write *T* (true) or *F* (false). Correct the false sentences.**

1. Grandma had to stay in hospital to rest.
2. Sadie was looking at her biology textbook when Mum came home.
3. After lunch the next day, everyone suggested ideas to cheer Grandma up.
4. Annette had to concentrate on her project for her photography exam.
5. Sadie and her friends stood under the lemon tree on the balcony.
6. Mum bought some new material from a stall in the market.
7. Annette told Grandma about the photography competition.
8. Everyone was impressed because Annette won the competition.
9. Annette decided she would like to go to art college.
10. Annette gave Grandma confidence.

2 **Think about the answers to these questions. Discuss your ideas.**

1. Why was Mum concerned about Grandma?
2. What sort of results do you think Sadie got in her exams? How do you know?
3. What job do you think Sadie might do in the future? Think of two words.
4. Why do you think Annette laughed when Grandma suggested that she enter one of her photos in the competition?
5. Why do you think Grandma was cheerful at the end of the story?
6. Which people helped each other in this story?
7. Who do you think helped the most in this story? Who do you think was helped the most?

3 **Underline the incorrect word in each sentence. Write the correct word.**

1. "<u>Terrific</u> news!" Mum sighed with relief as she put down the phone. *Tremendous*
2. Mum was pleased because Grandma's opera was successful. _____
3. Sadie's report was about the Centre for Medical Sciences. _____
4. Dad got tickets for a concert at the theatre. _____
5. Sadie got her exam results in a clean, white envelope. _____
6. Annette gave Grandma a book of photographs. _____
7. There was a photography competition at the art studio. _____
8. Everyone was depressed when Annette got third prize. _____

4 **For each of these words, find one synonym and one antonym from the box.**

| depressed   terrible   beaming |
| worried   tremendous   relieved |

1. concerned _____ _____
2. radiant _____ _____
3. marvellous _____ _____

Your views

- What do you think Annette learned from talking to her Grandma?
- Do you talk to your grandparents? What do you talk about?
- Who helps you at home if you have a problem?

Working with words

A Language development
Adjectival phrases: reminder

Remember, a phrase is a group of words that makes sense. It does not express a complete idea on its own.

In Unit 2, you read simple adjectival phrases:
*He was almost hidden by a group of tourists **with clicking cameras**.*
*A **blue and gold** flag was flying above the vast entrance.*

- Phrases do not have a complete verb.
- An **adjectival phrase** tells you more about a **noun**.
- It adds **extra information** to the sentence in a few words.

Extra information in clauses

- A **clause** is a longer group of words with a complete verb. It can tell you more about the subject.

1 Read this example from the story.

"Isn't Grandma all right?" asked Sadie, glancing up from her chemistry text book.

- The clause **describes** Sadie. It tells the reader about Sadie when she asked the question. It does not have a complete verb. It uses the **present participle** but it is **not** a sentence.
- The sentence from the story can be rewritten as two sentences.

"Isn't Grandma all right?" asked Sadie. She glanced up from her chemistry text book.

What is the difference in meaning between these two sentences and the first sentence?

Clue: Which tells you the actions in a clear order? Which tells you about two actions happening at the same time?

Think about it: Why does a writer sometimes use a clause instead of starting a new sentence?

2 Read these sentences. Rewrite each sentence as two sentences.
1 They stood next to Mum's little lemon tree on the balcony, crying, laughing and hugging each other.

2 Over the next few weeks, Annette kept her camera with her all the time, ready for every opportunity.

B Making new words
Suffix -ous

- The suffix -ous can be added to some nouns to make adjectives.
  marvel   marvell**ous**   fame   fam**ous**

1 What do you think the spelling rule for adding -ous to nouns ending -e is? Write it.

_____

_____

2 Add -ous to these nouns. Write the complete adjective.

1 nerve _____   2 ridicule _____

Look out!

courage   cour**ag**eous

Watch out for this one, too!

gorgeous

3 Look at this noun that ends -y and the adjective. Write the spelling rule.

fury   furious

_____

_____

4 Add -ous to these words. Check you understand them.

1 vary _____   2 glory _____

C Spelling
Words ending -er and -re

- Some words in English end -er. A few words end -re. The endings sound the same.
  *"Did you tell her my teach**er** has chosen my report on the Cent**re** for Biological Sciences?"*

1 Read and learn these words. Check you know what they mean.

met**re**   lit**re**   theat**re**   somb**re**   fib**re**

2 Think of four nouns that end -er.

Grammar

1 **Read.**

Annette **has been interested** in photography **for** a long time. She **has been taking photos since** her seventh birthday when her grandma gave her a little camera. Today Annette is working on her photography project. In fact, **she has been working** on it all week. She **has kept** her camera with her at all times, ready for every opportunity. She **has taken** a lot of photos of her family and her friends.

This morning she is in the park. She **has been** here **since** nine o'clock but she **has not taken** many photos. It **has been raining for** the last ten minutes and Annette **has been sheltering** under a tree. She **has been waiting** patiently for the rain to stop. Suddenly, she spots two boys on bikes. They **have been cycling** in the rain. They are completely wet but they are laughing. Quickly Annette raises her camera and presses the button. She **has** just **taken** the picture which will win third prize in the photography competition.

2 **Answer these questions.**
1. How long has she been taking photos?
2. What has Annette been doing all week?
3. What has she kept with her at all times?
4. How long has she been in the park?
5. How long has it been raining?
6. What have the two boys been doing?

3 **Make sentences. Use the present perfect simple.**
1. Annette – be – park – nine o'clock
   Annette has been in the park since nine o'clock.
2. She – just – take – photo
3. Oh, no! – boys – break – window
4. My grandparents – live – abroad – years
5. Look! – Someone – steal – statue
6. Look! – wind – blow down – trees

Remember!
We use the present perfect simple:
1. for actions that happened at an indefinite time in the past.
   *My uncle **has been** to China.*
2. when something started in the past and still continues now.
   *We **have lived** here for three years.*
3. when the result of a past action is visible now.
   *Oh, no! I**'ve broken** my sunglasses!*

- Find examples of 1, 2 and 3 in Activity 3 above. Think of more examples of 1, 2 and 3.

4 **Make sentences. Use the present perfect continuous. Use *for* or *since*.**
1. It – rain – eight hours.
   It has been raining for eight hours.
2. Annette – take – photos – her seventh birthday
3. Annette – stand – under – tree – ten minutes
4. We – study – English – several years
5. Professor James – teach – science – 1984
6. The players – train – hard – January
7. I – revise – exams – three weeks
8. You – watch – TV – too long

Remember!
We use the present perfect continuous:
1. when an action started in the past and is still continuing now.
   *Lisa **has been talking** on the phone for hours.*
   We often use a time phrase to show how long the action has been continuing:
   *... **since** three o'clock, ... **for** a long time.*
2. when the result of a past action is visible now and that action continued for some time.
   *Meg's eyes are red. I think she**'s been crying**.*

- Think of some more examples of 1 and 2 above.

Grammar in use 10

Portrait Project
Town Fair
Morris dancing
Jack, Ross, Laura
Video and interviews

1 🎧 Listen and read.

Ross: Hello! Today we're at our annual Town Fair.
Laura: There are stalls selling all sorts of things like home-made cakes, sweets and toys.
Ross: And there are stalls where you can play games and win a prize.
Laura: There are pony rides, too, and a fancy dress competition for both children and adults.
Ross: The Hampton Hippos are going to give a demonstration of their basketball skills.
Laura: And I'm really excited because later on there's going to be Morris dancing.
Ross: **Have** you **ever tried** Morris dancing, Laura?
Laura: No, I**'ve never tried** it. Actually, it's usually men who do Morris dancing, isn't it?
Ross: That's right. And in fact my Uncle Jim is dancing here this afternoon. He **joined** the Hampton Morris Men last summer. I'm going to interview him later.
Laura: What do the Morris Men wear when they're dancing?
Ross: They wear white shirts and trousers with bells and ribbons on them. **Haven't** you **ever seen** Morris dancing?
Laura: No, I**'ve never seen** it. **Have** you?
Ross: Yes, I saw the Hampton Morris Men two weeks ago. It's good fun. And the music's brilliant.
Laura: Do they dance to a live band? What instruments do they play?
Ross: There's an accordion, a flute, drums and a fiddle.
Laura: Oh, listen! The band's just starting up! This is really exciting!
Ross: Jack, make sure you film it all, OK?

2 Answer these questions.

1. What can you do at the Town Fair?
2. Why are the Hampton Hippos there?
3. Who is Ross going to interview? Why?
4. What do Morris dancers wear?
5. Has Laura ever seen Morris dancing?
6. Has Ross ever seen it?
7. When did he see it?
8. Did he like it? Why?

3 Ask and answer.

1. see – a Morris dancer?
   A: Have you ever seen a Morris dancer?
   B: Yes, I have. / No, I haven't. I've never seen one.
2. ride – a pony?
3. enter – a competition?
4. be – to a fair?
5. win – a prize?
6. hear – a live band?
7. play – an accordion?
8. eat – a home-made cake?

4 Ask and answer questions about Ross and Laura.

1. Ross – see – Morris dancing? (two weeks ago)
   A: Has Ross ever seen Morris dancing?
   B: Yes, he has.
   A: When did he see it?
   B: He saw it two weeks ago.
2. Ross – meet – Professor Bolt? (last month)
3. Laura – make – a cake? (yesterday)
4. Ross – play – basketball? (on Saturday)
5. Laura – lose – her camera? (last year)
6. Ross – draw – a portrait? (three weeks ago)

Remember!
When an action happened at an indefinite time in the past, we use the present perfect.
*Joe **has taken** lots of interesting photos.*
When an action happened at a definite time in the past, we use the past simple.
*He **took** an amazing photo yesterday.*

Grammar extra p130

Grammar in use: *ever* and *never*; present perfect vs. past simple; Grammar extra: phrasal verbs with *go*   103

Writing

Features of story plots

> What happens in a story is called the **plot**.
> Usually, the plot has a **beginning**, a **middle** and an **end**.
> The story is told from the beginning to the end.

▶ **The plot**

The plot of *A helping hand* is about one family over a period of time.

What part of the story?	How do you know time has passed?	What happens?
Beginning		Grandma had a successful operation.
	Next evening …	Mum visited Grandma who felt lonely and depressed.
	At lunch next day …	The family thought of things to cheer Grandma up.
Middle	Over the next few weeks …	Annette took lots of photographs.
	Four weeks later …	Annette gave Grandma an album of her photographs. Grandma suggested Annette enters one for a photography competition.
End	A month later …	Annette won third prize in the competition.
	Later that day …	Annette decided she would go to college and study photography.

▶ **Past tenses**

Stories are usually written in the **past tenses**.

Mum **sighed** with relief …

I**'ve been revising** …

Everyone **was** pleased …

▶ **Dialogue**

Stories usually have **dialogue**.

'Isn't Grandma all right?' asked Sadie …

'She feels lonely,' Mum said.

ACTIVITY

Rewrite the following dialogue, **setting it out** and **punctuating** it correctly.

You came third? That's wonderful said Grandma. I'm so pleased said Annette. I didn't think I had a chance. Well said Mum you never know how good you are until you try. I think it's fantastic said Sadie. I have to thank Grandma said Annette. Her encouragement gave me the confidence to enter. Well done, Grandma said Sadie.

Writing

Writing together

> Mum, Dad, Sadie and Annette planned a surprise birthday party for Grandma's 80th birthday. They had a week to plan the party. As a class you are going to write the **story** of the surprise birthday party.

1. Think about the beginning, middle and end of the party.

   Beginning: Planning the party
   - What day did the family start planning the party?
   - What did they talk about?
   - What jobs had to be done?

   Middle: Everyone prepares for the party. This takes place over a week.
   - What did Annette do? When did she do it?
   - What did Sadie do? When did she do it?
   - What did Mum do? When did she do it?
   - What did Dad do? When did he do it?

   > **Here are some useful time phrases you could use:**
   >
   > Early that morning … Later that day …
   > In the morning / afternoon / evening …
   > Next day … After breakfast / lunch / dinner …
   > The day before / after …

   End: The day of the party
   - What still had to be done in the morning?
   - When did the guests arrive?
   - When did Grandma open her presents?
   - When did they cut the cake?
   - When did everyone eat / dance / play party games?
   - When did the party end?

2. Write the story.

Indivdual writing (WB p89)

Listening and speaking

Conversation practice

1 Holly and Jack are talking. Look at the pictures and the words in the box. What do you think they are talking about?

> Have you seen …? Haven't you ever seen …? I've been to … I've never been to …
> festival ceremony costume colourful parade carnival fireworks new year dragon

  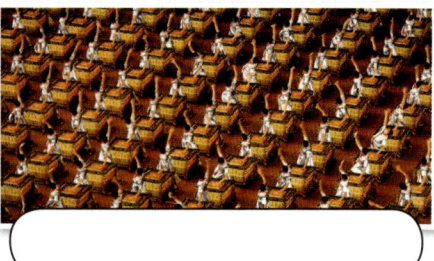

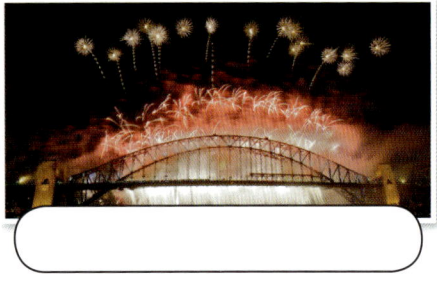 

2 🎧 2.15 Listen to Holly and Jack. Were you right?

3 Write these captions underneath the pictures.

New Year, Sydney, Australia Olympic Games, Beijing, China Carnival, Rio, Brazil
Spring Fair, Spain Chinese New Year, Hong Kong

4 🎧 2.15 Read the phrases in the box. Then listen again and spot the phrases.

> Let's have a look. You're right. Lucky them!
> What on earth are they doing? That's awesome! Oh, I get it!

5 Talk to a friend about the pictures. Have you ever seen celebrations like these? Use some of the phrases if you can. Start like this: *Look at this picture! It's great.*

Listening comprehension

1 🎧 2.16 Listen to a conversation. Which festival are the people at?

2 🎧 2.16 Read the questions. Then listen again and answer the questions.

1 How many times has the woman been to the festival?
2 Which costumes does she like best?
3 When did the first festival take place?
4 How long does it last?
5 What is the man most interested in?
6 Why does he want to see some traditional dancing?

3 Would you like to go to this festival? Why? / Why not?

Individual speaking

You are going to talk about a festival you have been to or a festival you know about. **WB p90**

106 Listening and speaking: conversation in pairs; listening comprehension; individual speaking

Sports reports

Check-in

People read sports reports to find out what happened in a game or match.

Are you interested in any sports? Which ones? Have you ever read a sports report? Which sport? Where else can you get news about sports? Think of three places.

You are going to read a sports report about a football match.

Reading

- Most **newspaper reports** use the **past tense**.
- A report has an eye-catching **headline**.
- The **first paragraph** says what the report is about.
- The events are usually written **in the order** they happened.
- The report contains **facts** and sometimes a **comment** in direct speech.

How is the text usually set out in a newspaper?

- These words are in the report.

  soar   stunt   descend   chauffeur   limousine
  roller skates   manager   jubilant   splendid

What do they mean? Check in your dictionary.

Vocabulary and spelling

- Learn words to do with **football**.
- Learn about **compound nouns** and **hyphens**.
- Learn about spelling **words with -tch**.

Grammar

- Practise **reported speech**.
- Practise **defining relative clauses**.
- Practise using **make** or **do**.

Writing

- Learn about the features of **newspaper and magazine writing**.
- Write a **sports report** of a football final.
- Write a **news report** about a person.

Listening

- Jack and Holly **talking about transport**.
- A **dialogue** in which Laura and Ross discuss travel.
- Station and airport **announcements**.

Speaking

- Talk to a friend about your **experiences of travel**.
- Tell the class about **a journey** you have made.

107

Reading

The Star

SPORTS

A match with a difference

by Star *sports correspondent, Andy Bridges*

National championship
City 1   United 2

1 **There was plenty of first class football to entertain the crowd of 50,000 that watched Saturday's semi-final between City and United. It's just what we've come to expect from these two giants of the game. What nobody expected, though, was the arrival in the stadium of United's new owner, businessman Fergal Flynn – by hot-air balloon.**

2 Half an hour before kickoff, the green and yellow striped balloon soared over the stadium. At first, most people thought it was an advertising stunt for Flynn Airlines but as the balloon sank lower and lower over the stadium, the waving figure of Flynn could be seen. Spectators watched in amazement as the balloon descended to the centre of the pitch, landing within a few metres of the centre spot. Long-time United fan Fred Usher told the Star, "I've never seen anything like it. You expect the new owner to turn up in a chauffeur-driven limousine, don't you?" Fifteen-year-old Jamie Usher commented, "Some people think that Mr Flynn's a bit of a show-off but he's the man who's going to invest in United. We hope he's going to buy in some new players. So long as we win the championship, I don't mind how he travels. He can come on roller skates if he likes."

3 While the ground staff were folding up the balloon, Mr Flynn addressed the spectators. He told them that he was pleased to be the new owner of United. He said that the new United colours would be green and yellow so they would match the green and yellow striped planes flown by Flynn Airlines. After that, Mr Flynn shook hands with the United team manager and team coach, then he went to his private viewing box.

Mr Fergal Flynn arriving by hot-air balloon

Mr Fergal Flynn, United's new owner

The match was full of drama from the kick-off. A swift pass from City's captain, Steve Amos, found Smith on the right wing. A long pass reached Dennis. He dodged his opponent and sent the ball across the goal where Amos slammed it straight to the back of the net. Strachan, the United goalkeeper, was nowhere near it. City fans were jubilant to take the lead after only 40 seconds. City didn't have time to relax though, as United equalised ten minutes later with a powerful header from King, off Benezi's cross.

With the score 1–1 at half-time, the spectators were entertained by the release of 2,000 green and yellow balloons. Each balloon carried United's fixtures list for the season and a 10% off voucher for Flynn airlines. Mr Flynn talked to reporters before play began again. He said that cheaper transport was important. He hoped that a lot of football fans would decide to fly with Flynn airlines in the future.

The second half began with some skilful football from both teams. Da Silva, City's new international player, justified his place in the team with a splendid swinging long shot. Strachan dived for it and made a spectacular save.

Towards the end of the half, the play became untidy. United forward, Dineen, got a yellow card for a clumsy tackle on Smith. Benezi got another for pulling Amos' shirt. He was lucky not to get a red card for a deliberate foul on Dennis.

King, newly returned from injury, was clearly tiring and was substituted after 35 minutes of the second half by reserve striker Billy Jones. Jones lost no time in making his mark, scoring the decider off a long ball from Walker.

Flynn should be pleased with his new club. United is the team that is the favourite to win the championship. One thing Flynn should know about football, though – it's much less predictable than an airline.

Reading comprehension

1 **Choose the best word to complete the statements.**

1. There was plenty of first class football to entertain the crowd that watched Saturday's _____.
   - a kick-off
   - b game
   - c semi-final
2. Spectators watched in amazement as the hot-air balloon descended to the centre of the _____.
   - a spot
   - b pitch
   - c stadium
3. While the ground staff were folding up the hot-air balloon, Mr Flynn addressed _____.
   - a the spectators
   - b the players
   - c the team manager
4. The new United colours will match the green and yellow _____.
   - a planes
   - b hot-air balloon
   - c airline
5. Strachan, the United _____, was nowhere near the ball.
   - a defender
   - b striker
   - c goalkeeper
6. Jones scored the _____ off a long ball from Walker.
   - a decider
   - b header
   - c goal
7. United is the team that is the favourite to win the _____.
   - a final
   - b championship
   - c competition

2 **Think about the answers to these questions. Discuss your ideas.**

1. Why do you think the headline was chosen?
2. Was the match a good one? How do you know?
3. What sort of person do you think Fergal Flynn is? How do you know?
4. Why should he be pleased with his new club?
5. Do you think the fans will be pleased with the new owner? Why? / Why not?

3 **What do these expressions mean? Discuss in pairs. Match them to the definitions.**

> semi-final   kick-off   half-time
> show-off   first class

1. of the best quality _____
2. a person who tries to present himself or herself as being clever or very successful _____
3. the first action in a football match _____
4. the period that divides two parts of a match _____
5. a match played between two of the last four teams in a competition _____

4 **Write the paragraph number that tells you …**

- a what happened between the first half and the second half of the match. ___
- b about the bad play late in the match. ___
- c about the new colours for United. ___
- d how Flynn should feel. ___
- e what nobody expected. ___
- f about the new international player. ___
- g what happened at the beginning of the first half. ___
- h who scored the deciding goal. ___
- i fans' comments about Fergal Flynn. ___

Your views

- Do you think Andy Bridges wrote a good report? Why? / Why not?
- Did Mr Flynn's arrival by balloon make the report more or less interesting? Why?
- Do you think Mr Flynn is a show-off or a clever businessman? Why?

Working with words

A Making new words

Compound nouns

> Sometimes two nouns can be put together to make a new noun.
> goal + keeper = goalkeeper
> foot + ball = football

1 Join these words and write the correct compound noun.

business + man = _____
air + line = _____

2 Read these definitions. Write the compound noun.

1. a bench for doing work on _____
2. a burger made of beef _____
3. the light of the sun _____
4. the place where two roads cross _____

3 Think of four compound nouns of your own.

_____
_____
_____
_____

Find some in your dictionary if you can't think of any.

Hyphenated words

> Sometimes words can be joined with a **hyphen** to make a new word. e.g. check-in

4 Read these words from the sports report. What part of speech are they?

semi-final   show-off   half-time

Hyphenated words as adjectives

> Sometimes the new word that is made is an adjective. It is used to describe a noun.
> e.g. half-time entertainment
> This means *an entertainment that happens in the period of time that divides two halves of a match.*

5 Read these examples.

a hot-air balloon   a long-time fan
a chauffeur-driven limousine

Check you understand what the phrases mean.

6 Answer these questions about the phrases.

1. How would each phrase be written if the hyphenated words were not used? Write it underneath.

   hot-air balloon
   _____

   chauffeur-driven limousine
   _____

   long-time fan
   _____

2. Why do you think words are sometimes joined with a hyphen?

B Spelling

Words with -tch

> Some words in English end -tch, sounding like ch.
> pi**tch** ma**tch** sti**tch** wa**tch**
> A few words have -tch- in the middle.

1 Complete these words. Write them next to the correct picture.

pi_ _ _er   sa_ _ _el   ki_ _ _en

1 _____

2 _____

3 _____

2 Read the definitions. Complete the words ending -tch.

1. to grab hold of _____ _tch
2. to go and get something _____ _tch
3. to break out of an egg _____ _tch

Grammar

1 Read.

When the crowd first saw the green and yellow striped hot-air balloon, they **thought** it **was** an advertising stunt for Flynn Airlines. Then someone **shouted** that the balloon **was landing** on the pitch.

One fan **commented** that Mr Flynn **was** a bit of a show-off. Another **said** that he **hoped** Flynn **would buy** in some new players. A third **added** that they **needed** a man like Fergal Flynn.

Before the match started, Mr Flynn addressed the spectators. He **told** them that he **loved** football and said that he **was** delighted to be the new owner of United. He **explained** that the new United colours **would be** green and yellow and **said** that they **would match** the green and yellow striped planes of Flynn Airlines.

2 Answer these questions.
1. What did people think when they saw the balloon?
2. What did someone shout?
3. What did the fans say about Fergal Flynn?
4. What did Mr Flynn say to the fans first?
5. What did he say about United's new colours?

3 Report these sentences. Use the words in brackets.
1. "United is a great team." (Mr Flynn said that …)
2. "The balloon is an advertising stunt." (The spectators thought that …)
3. "The balloon is landing on the pitch." (A man shouted that …)
4. "The club needs new players." (One fan commented that …)
5. "The new colours will be green and yellow." (Mr Flynn explained that …)

4 Interview Mr Flynn. Ask and answer in pairs. Make notes.
1. What do you think of United?
2. What do you think of the City players?
3. How do you feel about being the new owner?

4. Why are you changing the club colours?
5. How many new players are you planning to buy?
6. Who will win the match?

Report what Mr Flynn said.

Remember!
In reported speech:
- when the reporting verb is in the past (He **said** that …, She **told** me that …) the verbs which were in the direct speech often change. Present tenses become past tenses:

"The watch **is** expensive." He said that the watch **was** expensive.
"The boys **walk** to school." He said that the boys **walked** to school.

will becomes *would*:
"The exams **will be** hard." He said that the exams **would be** hard.

- subject pronouns can change.
"**I** am ill," he said. He said that **he** was ill.
"**You** are early," he told the girl. He told the girl that **she** was early.

Always think of the meaning of the sentences and you won't go wrong!

Grammar: reported speech (changes in tenses and pronouns)

Grammar in use

11

Portrait Project
Transport
Jack and Holly
Write report, take photos

1 🎧 2.18 Listen and read.

Holly: Why do we have to write a report about transport?
Jack: Because a good transport system is something **that**'s very important for a town.
Holly: Have we got a good transport system in Hampton?
Jack: It's getting better, I think. A few years ago, the traffic was terrible in the centre of town. There was a lot of pollution from cars and lorries. It was very noisy, too.
Holly: So it's better now?
Jack: Definitely. There are some streets **where** cars are banned.
Holly: You mean the pedestrian areas.
Jack: Yes, that's right. And last year the 'Park and ride' scheme started. People can leave their cars at a big car park on the ring road and get onto buses **which** take them into the centre of town.
Holly: There are more cycle lanes as well, aren't there?
Jack: Yes, there are. It's not dangerous to cycle in town anymore.
Holly: So there's less traffic in the centre now.
Jack: Yes, but it's still quite busy at the times **when** people are going to and from work.
Holly: You mean the rush hour.
Jack: Exactly. There are always traffic jams early in the morning and in the afternoon.
Holly: We should write about the new railway station, too.
Jack: Yes, and there are lots of people **who** live in Hampton and work in London. Most of them travel by train.
Holly: My dad commutes to London every day. We could interview him.
Jack: An interview with a commuter. Good idea!

2 Answer these questions.

1. Is the transport system in Hampton good or bad?
2. How does a 'Park and ride' scheme work?
3. What are 'pedestrian areas'?
4. What is a 'ring road'?
5. What is the 'rush hour'?
6. What are 'commuters'?

3 Find the correct endings. Write the letters.

1. A good transport system is something ___
2. There are many people in Hampton ___
3. The rush hour is the time ___
4. The station car park is the place ___
5. In the centre of town there are streets ___

a. when people are going to and from work.
b. which is very important for a town.
c. that are closed to cars and lorries.
d. where commuters leave their cars.
e. that commute to London every day.

4 Ask and answer. Use the phrases in the box.

> the time when   a part of the road which
> people that   a road that   a person who
> a place where   a line of cars which

1. a cycle lane
   A: What's a cycle lane?
   B: It's a part of the road which is only used by cyclists.
2. the rush hour   3. a traffic jam   4. a car park
5. a pedestrian   6. commuters   7. a ring road

Remember!

In relative clauses:
- *which* or *that* refers to things or animals.
  The film **which / that** I saw was great.
- *who* or *that* refers to people.
  That's the boy **who / that** found the ring.
- *where* refers to a place; *when* refers to a time.
  This is the town **where** I was born.
  August is the month **when** we go on holiday.

- Think of more sentences like those above.

Grammar extra p130

Writing

Features of newspapers and magazines

> We read newspapers and magazines to find out what is happening in the world. You have read a **sports report** about a football match.

▶ **Headline**

The headline is very important. If readers find the headline interesting, they will read the article.

A match with a difference

ACTIVITY
1. Would this **headline** make you read the article? Why? Why not?
2. Read these **headlines**. What do you think each sports report is about?

United 6-0 disaster   World Cup Mystery   Olympic Gold for Russia

▶ **By-line**

The by-line is the name of the person who wrote the article.   *Andy Bridges*

▶ **Past tenses**

Most newspaper reports are written about events that have happened. They are written in **past tenses**.

> The match **was** full of drama from the kickoff.
>
> King ... **was** substituted after 35 minutes.

ACTIVITY Find five more examples of **past tenses** in the report.

▶ **Opening paragraph**

The headline has made readers want to read the article. The **opening paragraph** must keep readers interested and let them know what the article is about.

> ... Saturday's semi-final between City and United.
>
> the arrival of United's owner ... by hot-air balloon.

▶ **Sequence of events**

Sports reports usually start at the **beginning** of the story and tell the reader what happens **in order**.

> Fergal Flynn arrived in a hot-air balloon
> match began
> first half
> half-time
> second half

▶ **Facts**

Newspaper articles report **facts**.

> the green and yellow striped balloon
>
> United equalised ten minutes later

ACTIVITY Find five more facts in the report.

▶ **Quotations**

Reporters often include what people think about what has happened. They **quote** the words actually spoken.

> "He can come on roller skates if he likes."

▶ **Illustrations**

A **drawing** or **photograph** makes a newspaper report more interesting.

Writing

Writing together

> United won the semi-final against City. United played Rangers in the final and won the championship. As a class you are going to write the **newspaper report** of the match.

1 Discuss these questions and make notes.
- What was the final score?
- Who scored the goals?
- Was anyone sent off?
- Did anyone play really well?
- Did anyone play really badly?
- Was there a penalty?
- Did anything unusual happen?
- Did the match go into extra time?

2 Sort your notes under these headings.

the first half   the half-time   the second half

3 Once you have made notes on the facts and when they happened, discuss the following.

The headline:
- It could include the final score or the name of a star player, or use your own ideas.

The opening paragraph:
- Let the readers know which teams were playing and what they were playing for.
- Was there a big crowd?
- Was it an exciting or dull match?

Quotes:
- The two managers were interviewed after the match.
- What did the winning manager say?
- What did the losing manager say?

4 Write your newspaper report.

> **Remember!**
> - Include the by-line.
> - Write in past tenses.

Individual writing WB p99

Listening and speaking

Conversation practice

1 Laura and Ross are talking. Look at the pictures and the words in the box. What do you think they are talking about?

> travel   fly   sail   flight   journey   stand up
> walk around   sit still   get stuck   carriage

2 🎧 2.19 Listen to Laura and Ross. Were you right?

3 🎧 2.19 Listen again. Who has travelled by these methods of transport? Laura? Ross? Anyone else?

4 Talk to a friend. Have you ever used these methods of transport? Start like this:

Tell me (name), have you ever flown in a plane?

Listening comprehension

1 🎧 2.20 Listen to some announcements. Where are they being made? (two places)

2 🎧 2.20 Look at the sentences. Then listen again and complete the information.

1 The first train is arriving at _____.
2 The second train is late because of _____.
3 The train will arrive _____ late.
4 Lucy Davies is waiting for _____.
5 BA flight 306 is going to _____ soon.
6 Passengers must keep their _____ with them.
7 If they don't, their luggage _____.
8 David Robertson has left his tickets at the _____.
9 Flight AA736 is going to _____.
10 Passengers will receive free drinks because of the _____.

Individual speaking

You are going to talk about a journey you have made by plane, by train or by car.   **WB p100**

On stage

12

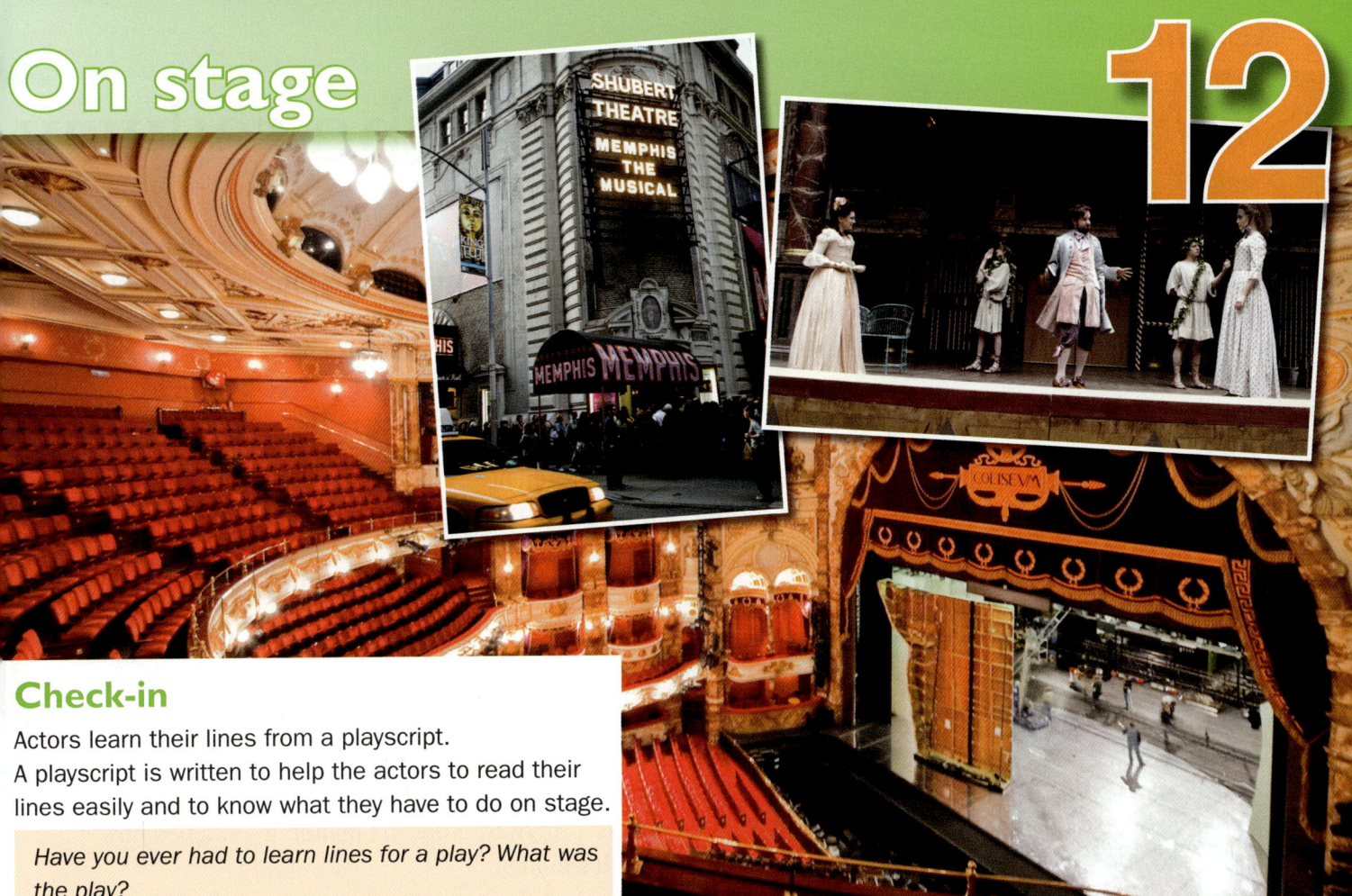

Check-in

Actors learn their lines from a playscript.
A playscript is written to help the actors to read their lines easily and to know what they have to do on stage.

Have you ever had to learn lines for a play? What was the play?
Do you think it is easy or difficult to learn lines?
Have you ever been in a play and forgotten your lines?
Do you enjoy watching plays? Why? / Why not?

You are going to read a scene from a playscript.

Reading
- The playscript lists **the characters** first.
- It says where **the scene** happens.
- The **actors' words** are set out on the line after the name of the character.

Does a playscript use speech marks?

- **Stage directions** tell the actors how to speak and what to do.
- These words are in the playscript.
  familiar   weird   slip   landslide   shocked   mound
  disaster   brainwave   urgently

What do they mean? Check in your dictionary.

Vocabulary and spelling
- Learn words to do with **a disaster**.
- Learn about **adverbial phrases** and the **suffix -ive**.
- Learn about spelling **words with *a* after *w***.

Grammar
- Practise the **second conditional**.
- Practise **have to** and **must** in questions and negative form.
- Practise **phrases with break**.

Writing
- Learn about the **features of a playscript**.
- Write the **next scene** for the playscript you read.
- Write a **new scene** for the same characters.

Listening
- Laura, Jack, Holly and Ross's **discussion** about their *Portrait* project entry.
- A **dialogue** about things Laura and Ross have to do.
- An **emailed letter**.

Speaking
- Talk with a friend about things you **have to do this week**.
- Tell the class about what you **have to do in the next few weeks**.

Reading

Danger on the railway

Events so far …
Roberta, Peter and Phyllis have moved from London and are living in the country. Their house is near a railway line and they have become familiar with the trains, the station and the people who work there. They often watch the trains go by and wave to the drivers and passengers. One day, they go to pick wild cherries from trees that grow on the sides of the steep valley where the railway runs.

Characters: Roberta, Peter, Phyllis
Scene: the railway line in the valley

ROBERTA: The cherry trees are growing best right down there, near the tunnel.
PETER: Let's go down the steps beside the tunnel. Then we can easily reach the cherries.
ROBERTA: Good idea. It's not far. Come on.
PHYLLIS: Wait a minute. Listen, what's that weird sound?
ROBERTA: (*thoughtfully*) It isn't the wind.
PETER: No … [*pause*] Anyway, it doesn't matter, it's stopped now.
PHYLLIS: No, listen. It's louder.
PETER: (*puzzled*) Look at that tree over there, it's moving!
ROBERTA: So it is! How strange! And so are the others.
PETER: It looks like the trees are walking down towards the railway line!
PHYLLIS: (*a little scared*) What's happening? Is it magic?
ROBERTA: No, it's not magic. The side of the valley is slipping. It's all coming down, the rocks, the earth, the trees, everything!
PETER: It's a landslide … straight onto the railway line!
ROBERTA: (*in a shocked voice*) Look at the huge mound it's made! It's massive!
PHYLLIS: It's right across the line!
PETER: (*worriedly*) And the 11.29 train hasn't gone by yet. We must let them know at the station straight away, or there's going to be a terrible disaster!
ROBERTA: (*starts running*) Let's run!
PETER: No, wait! There's no time! It's ten miles away and it's past eleven o'clock now.
PHYLLIS: Couldn't we climb up a telegraph post and do something to the wires?
PETER: We don't know how.
PHYLLIS: They do it in war. I know, I've heard of it.
PETER: They only cut them, silly, and that won't do any good.
ROBERTA: And we wouldn't be able to cut them even if we got up there.
PETER: If only we had something red, we could wave to the train.

118 Reading: a playscript

PHYLLIS:	We could wave, anyway.
ROBERTA:	They'd only think it was us, as usual. We've waved so often before. Oh, what can we do?
PETER:	We must go down to the line, at least. This way. [*The children climb down the hill.*]
PHYLLIS:	Oh, how hot I am and I thought it was going to be cold. I wish we hadn't put on … (*excitedly*) our flannel petticoats!
ROBERTA:	Oh! … Yes! They're red! Let's take them off.
PETER:	What a brainwave! Phyllis, give me your petticoat. Thanks. Now … I'll have to tear it.
PHYLLIS:	Tear it? You mustn't!
PETER:	(*firmly*) Shut up, Phyllis! In this situation, we have to be inventive!
ROBERTA:	Oh, yes, tear them into little bits if you like. Don't you see, Phil, if we can't stop the train, there'll be a real live accident, with people killed. Oh, horrible!
PETER:	There, now we've got six flags. And we've got seven minutes. We have to have flagpoles. Snap off these long thin branches … hurry.
PHYLLIS:	We'll have to cut holes in the flags and run the sticks through the holes.
ROBERTA:	Yes! Quickly! There! Now I'll push these two flags into the stones under the sleepers, right in the middle of the track. There, that's done!
PETER:	You two can have a flag each and I'll have the other two because it was my idea to wave something red.
PHYLLIS:	(*annoyed*) They're our petticoats, though …
ROBERTA:	(*anxiously*) Oh, what does it matter who waves what, if only we can save the train?
PETER:	It should be here by now.
PHYLLIS:	I expect your watch is wrong and the train's already gone by.
ROBERTA:	No, I can hear it in the distance.
PHYLLIS:	Oh, yes you're right, it's coming. (*excitedly*) It's coming at top speed!
PETER:	Stand firm and wave like mad. When it gets to that big bush, step back but go on waving.
PHYLLIS:	It's getting closer … wave your flags, we must wave! [*The children wave their flags.*]
ROBERTA:	(*urgently*) They won't see us. They won't see us … it's all no good!
PHYLLIS:	It's coming closer!
PETER:	(*in a loud voice*) Keep off the line, Roberta, you silly cuckoo!
PHYLLIS:	They have to see us, they have to!
ROBERTA:	It's no good. It isn't stopping!
PETER:	(*shouting*) Stand back!
ROBERTA:	(*desperately*) Not yet, not yet! … Oh, stop, stop, stop!
PETER AND PHYLLIS:	(*shouting*) Roberta!!

Reading comprehension

1 **Answer these questions.**
1. What did Roberta, Peter and Phyllis often do?
2. Why did they go to the valley on that day?
3. What was the first unusual event?
4. What strange thing happened next?
5. What really happened?
6. What did the children decide they must do? Why?
7. Why couldn't they go to the station?
8. What ideas did Roberta and Phyllis have?
9. What idea did Peter have?
10. How did the children make the red flags?

2 **Think about the answers to these questions. Discuss your ideas.**
1. Why do you think Phyllis thought they were seeing something magic when the trees moved?
2. What did the children think would happen to the train if they couldn't stop it?
3. Which of the children do you think had the most important idea for trying to stop the train? What was it?
4. How did Phyllis feel about Peter having two flags? Why?
5. Do you think they managed to stop the train? What do you think happened at the end of the scene?

3 **Which words have the same, or similar, meanings? Match and list the pairs.**

| accident | anxiously | weird | disaster | desperately | slide |
| urgently | strange | slip | worriedly |

_____   _____   _____   _____   _____
_____   _____   _____   _____   _____

4 **Who said these words? Scan the text and write the name.**
1. What's that weird sound? _____
2. Is it magic? _____
3. The side of the valley is slipping. _____
4. We must let them know at the station … _____
5. They do it in war. _____
6. Oh, what can we do?
7. … I thought it was going to be cold. _____
8. What a brainwave! _____
9. We have to have flagpoles. _____
10. They're our petticoats, though … _____
11. It's coming at top speed! _____
12. Stand firm and wave like mad. _____
13. Keep off the line … _____
14. They have to see us … _____
15. It isn't stopping! _____

Your views
- If you were with the children trying to stop the train, would you do anything differently? What would you do differently? Why?
- Do you think what they were trying to do was a bit dangerous or so dangerous that they should not have done it?
- Did they do the right thing? Why?

Working with words 12

A Language development
Adverbial phrases

- An adverbial phrase is a group of words that makes sense. It does not contain a complete verb.
- It is part of a sentence. It adds extra information.
- They can tell us about the **time** or **place** that something happens.

1 Look at the underlined phrase in this sentence. Does the extra information tell you about the *time* or the *place* that the trees are walking? Write the correct word after the phrase.

It looks like the trees are walking down towards the railway line. _____

2 In the sentence below, does the underlined phrase tell you about the *time* the train should be here, or the *place*? Write the correct word after the phrase.

The train should be here by now. _____

- These phrases tell us more about the actions: **where** and **when**. They are called **adverbial phrases**.
- An adverbial phrase can also tell us *how* an action is done.
  It's coming at top speed!

3 Read these sentences. Look at the phrases. Decide whether they tell you about the *time*, the *place* or *how* the action happens. Write the correct word after the phrases.

1. We must let them know at the station **straight away**. _____
2. Stand firm and wave **like mad**. _____
3. I can hear it **in the distance**. _____

B Making new words
Suffix -ive

- We can make some verbs into adjectives by adding *-ive*.
  *In this situation, we have to be invent**ive**!*

1 Read these verbs. Write the word again and add the suffix *-ive*.

1. act _____
2. protect _____
3. impress _____
4. possess _____
5. attract _____

What do the new words mean?

Check in your dictionary if you aren't sure.

C Spelling
a after *w* sounding *o*

- In some words with *a* after *w*, the *a* sounds like *o* in *spot*.
  *I expect your **watch** is wrong.*

1 Read and say these words. Check you understand them.

wash want warrior wander waft

a after *w* sounding *aw*

- In some words with *a* after *w*, the *a* sounds like *aw* in *claw*.
  *It looks like the trees are **walking** …*

2 Read and say these words. Check you understand them.

war water warm wall ward

3 Find the correct words on this page to match these definitions.

1. a room in a hospital where sick people are cared for _____
2. to walk slowly and without a clear direction _____
3. to float gently in the air _____
4. a time of fighting between armies _____

Grammar

1 Read.

Roberta, Peter and Phyllis are near the railway line. There has been a landslide and a huge mound of earth is covering the railway line. This is a dangerous situation. If a train **came** along the line now, it **would crash** into the mound of earth. If it **crashed** into the mound of earth, that **would be** a disaster. Many passengers **would be injured** or even killed if there **was** an accident.

What can they do? If the station **was** nearer, they **would be able to run** there and warn the people there but the station is ten miles away. They must do something – and quickly! Peter says, "If we **had** something red, we **could wave** to the train. Red means danger." Peter is right. If the train driver **saw** a red flag, he **would know** that something was wrong. Suddenly, Roberta has an idea. "Phyllis and I are wearing red petticoats," she says. "If we **took** them off, we **could make** them into flags!" What a brilliant idea!

2 Answer these questions.
1. What is covering the railway line?
2. If a train came along the line now, what would happen?
3. Is the station nearby?
4. If the station was nearby, what would they be able to do?
5. What are Phyllis and Roberta wearing?
6. If they took off their petticoats, what could they do?

3 Find the correct endings. Write the letters.
1. It would be a disaster ___
2. If there was an accident, ___
3. If they could run to the station, ___
4. They would be able to warn the train driver ___
5. If the driver saw a red flag, ___
6. The girls would be able to make red flags ___

a they would be able to warn someone.
b if they took off their petticoats.
c if the train crashed into the mound of earth.
d he would know that the train was in danger.
e many people would be injured.
f if they waved something red.

4 Look! The sentences have the same meaning.

*If they had a red flag, they **would be able to** warn the train driver.*

*If they had a red flag, they **could** warn the train driver.*

Change the sentences. Use *could*.
1. If the children ran to the station, they would be able to tell someone.
2. If they waved red flags, they would be able to warn the train driver.
3. If the girls took off their petticoats, they would be able to make red flags.

Change the sentences. Use *would be able to*.
4. If they lived by the sea, they could swim every day.
5. If Joe trained harder, he could play in the school team.
6. If the weather was fine, we could have a picnic.

> **Remember!**
> - In second conditional sentences we are talking about the present time.
>   *I haven't got a lot of money.*
>   *If I **had** a lot of money, I **would travel** round the world.*
> - Use the past tense after *if*. Use *would* + verb in the main clause.
> - In the main clause *would be able to* can be replaced by *could*.
>   *If he **went** to China, he **would be able to** learn Chinese.*
>   *If he **went** to China, he **could** learn Chinese.*

- Think of some more second conditional sentences.

Grammar in use

Portrait Project
Completing the Portrait project
Final meeting
Jack, Laura, Ross, Holly

1 🎧 **Listen and read.**

Jack: So, we've finished the project.
Holly: At last!
Ross: It was a lot of hard work but I think it looks great.
Laura: Hampton looks such an interesting place to live!
Jack: Laura's put everything on a DVD.
Holly: Well done, Laura!
Laura: Thanks. Ross helped me. We **had to** edit the videos.
Ross: That was tricky. We've added music here and there, too.
Holly: Lovely! So what are we doing today?
Ross: Today we **have to** check everything. We **have to** make sure that there are no mistakes.
Jack: When **do** we **have to** send it off?
Laura: The closing date of the competition is the 31st so we**'ll have to** post it soon.
Holly: We **must** remember to make a copy before we send it off.
Ross: Absolutely! We **mustn't** lose all our hard work.
Holly: What do you like best about our entry?
Jack: Some of the photos are fantastic.
Laura: I like the interview with Professor Bolt, the astronomer.
Holly: And the picture which Ross drew of him was brilliant.
Jack: I wonder if we'll win.
Ross: Who knows? What we **must** do now is cross our fingers and hope for the best.

2 **Answer these questions.**
1 What did Ross and Laura have to do?
2 What do they have to do today?
3 When will they have to post their entry?
4 What must they remember to do? Why?
5 What must they do now?

3 **Look at this page from Laura's diary. Today is Thursday.**

Monday	Dentist
Tuesday	Finish art project
Wednesday	Revise for maths exam
Thursday	Get to school early (maths exam)
Friday	Make birthday cake
Saturday	Shopping centre with Jack – buy Mum's birthday present
Sunday	Mum's birthday! Make sure she has a nice day!

4 **Answer these questions.**
1 Where – have to – go – Monday
   A: Where did she have to go on Monday?
   B: She had to go to the dentist.
2 What – have to – do – Tuesday
3 What – have to – do – yesterday
4 What – must – do – today
5 What – have to – do – tomorrow
6 Where – Jack and Laura – have to – go – Saturday
7 What – must – Jack and Laura – do – Sunday

Remember!
- In affirmative sentences *have to* and *must* have the same meaning.
  You **have to** work hard. You **must** work hard.
  (It is necessary to work hard.)
- In questions *have to* and *must* have the same meaning: **Do** you **have to** go? **Must** you go?
- In negative sentences *have to* and *must* have different meanings.
  You **do not have to leave** now. (It is not necessary to.)
  You **must not** leave now. (You are forbidden to.)

- Think of some more sentences with *have to* and *must*.

Grammar extra p130

Grammar in use: *must* and *have to*; Grammar extra: phrasal verbs with *break*

Writing

Features of playscripts

> **Playscripts** are the words actors must learn before they perform in front of an audience.

▶ **Characters**

A playscript begins with a list of the **characters** in the play.

> Roberta, Peter, Phyllis

▶ **Scene**

The **scene** is where the action takes place.

> The railway line in the valley

▶ **Layout**

The **layout of a playscript** is important. The **names of the characters** who are speaking are on the left in capitals.

> ROBERTA:

What the characters say – the **dialogue** – is written next to each name.

> ROBERTA: It isn't the wind.

Dialogue in playscripts does not have speech marks.

ACTIVITY
Set out this conversation as a **playscript**.
"What shall we do today?" asked Phyllis.
"I don't know," replied Roberta.
"We could just stay indoors," said Peter. "It looks cold out there."
Roberta said, "That's boring. We can't stay in all day."
"I know," said Phyllis, "let's go down to the railway line and pick wild cherries."

▶ **Stage directions**

There are two types of **stage directions** in the script.
These stage directions show how a character says the words and what he / she does when speaking.

> ROBERTA: (*starts running*) Let's run!
>
> PETER: (*in a loud voice*) Keep off the line, Roberta, you silly cuckoo!

This stage direction shows what the characters do when they are not speaking.

> [*The children climb down the hill.*]

ACTIVITY Find one or more example of each type of stage direction.

Writing

Writing together

> The train driver and his assistant get on the train and set off. They have no idea of the danger ahead. As a class you are going to write the **scene** from when they set off to when they see the children.

1 **Discuss these questions and make notes.**
- Who are the characters in the scene?
- Where is the scene set?
- What might be happening when the train is:
  in the station?   ready to set off?
- What might the train driver and his assistant talk about BEFORE they see the children?
  Remember: They have made this journey hundreds of times. They think this is just another ordinary day.
- What might they say when they see the children?
  Remember: They cannot see the mound blocking the line. They can only see the children waving the red flags.

2 **Write the dialogue.**

Think about:
- where the train is at the beginning of the scene
- where it goes to
- where it stops.

3 **Add stage directions to show how a character says and does things.**

> Here are some useful words and phrases you could use:
> *happily   cheerily   loudly   in a puzzled voice   alarmed   yelling*

Individual writing WB p107

Listening and speaking

Conversation practice

1. Laura, Jack, Holly and Ross are at Ross's house. Look at the pictures and the words in the box. What do you think they are talking about?

> have to   don't have to   will have to   must   shopping centre
> go shopping   dentist   hairdresser's   phone   email

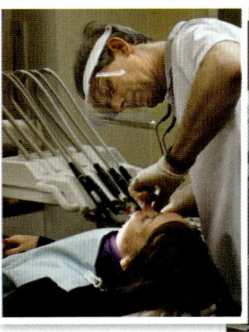

Hi, Dad!
Thanks for your email and the photos. They're great. It looks like you're having a really good time. When do you think you'll be coming home?

2. Listen to Laura and Ross. Were you right?

3. Read the phrases in the box. Then listen again and spot the phrases.

> Poor you/him/her!   Lucky you/him/her!   Me, too.   I'm not sure.
> What/How about you?   anything special   nothing special   Guess what!

4. Talk with your friends about the things that you have to do this week. Use some of the phrases in the box if you can. Start like this: *So … (name), what are you doing this week?*

Listening comprehension

1. Listen to Ross.
   He's going to read out the email which he has just received from Professor Brown, the organiser of the *Portrait* project. What do you think the email will say?

2. Read the sentences. Then listen again and write *T* (true) or *F* (false).
   1. Ross, Laura, Jack and Holly have not won the competition. ___
   2. There were one hundred entries in the competition. ___
   3. Many were of a low standard. ___
   4. They can feel proud of themselves. ___
   5. The *Portrait* project has been happening only in the UK. ___
   6. Teams from many countries will go to New York. ___
   7. The young people will have to pay for their own flights and hotels. ___
   8. They will be able to meet young people from other countries. ___

3. Compare your answers with those of your friends. Correct the false sentences.

4. Talk about it.
   1. What do you think about the email from Professor Brown?
   2. What do you think about the *Portrait of our town* project? Would you like to do a project like that?

Individual speaking

You are going to talk about all the things that you had to do last week, the things that you have to do this week and the things that you will have to do next week.

Grammar extra

make or *do*?

1 Complete the sentences using *make* or *do*.
1. We should _____ a list.
2. We're going to _____ a project about our town.
3. It's time to _____ a decision.
4. Jack doesn't want to _____ his homework.
5. It's great to _____ new friends.

2 Write and say. Make your own sentences with *make* or *do* and these words.

> friends   a list   homework   a decision   a project

Strawberry? Vanilla? Chocolate?

I don't know. What about banana?

Make up a sentence about the picture using *make*.

make or *take*?

1 Complete the sentences using *make* or *take*.
1. Don't look at him! Don't _____ any notice of him!
2. I _____ some photos of the elegant buildings.
3. The thieves _____ their escape down a dark street.
4. Are you going to _____ a holiday this year?
5. Well done! You've _____ no mistakes!

2 Write and say. Make your own sentences with *make* or *take* and these words.

> a mistake   a photo   a holiday
> his/her/its escape   any notice

Look at me! Look at me! Look at me!

Make up a sentence about the picture using *take*.

Let's look at *catch*!

1 Can you explain what these phrases mean?
1. The scientists are hoping to **catch a glimpse of** the sea otter.
2. He went walking in the rain and **caught a cold**.
3. If you hurry, you will **catch the train**.
4. The sun was so hot that the dry grass **caught fire**.
5. A pair of red shoes in the shop window **caught Sue's eye**.

2 Think of your own sentences using:

> catch a glimpse of   catch a cold / an illness   catch fire
> catch a train / a bus   catch someone's eye

Stop!

Make up a sentence about the picture using *catch*.

Grammar extra **127**

4

Let's look at bring!

1 **Can you explain what these phrases mean?**
   1 The astronauts went to the moon and **brought back** some moon rocks.
   2 Mr and Mrs Day **brought up** their children to be honest and kind to others.
   3 My father did not want to get a puppy but in the end we **brought** him **round**.
   4 That phone company **is bringing out** a new kind of mobile.
   5 Our teacher **brought forward** our test from Friday to Monday.

2 **Think of your own sentences using:**

   bring back   bring up   bring round   bring out   bring forward

Home at last

Make up a sentence about the picture using *bring*.

5

Let's take a look at look!

1 **Can you explain what these phrases mean?**
   1 Joe didn't understand the word so he **looked** it **up** in his dictionary.
   2 Dad is **looking for** his car keys. He can't find them anywhere.
   3 If you have a pet, you must **look after** it properly.
   4 The police are **looking into** the crime.
   5 **Look out!** That tree is going to fall!

2 **Think of your own sentences using:**

   look up   look for   look after   look into   look out

Where are my glasses?

Make up a sentence about the picture using *look*.

6

Let's look at stand!

1 **Can you explain what these phrases mean?**
   1 The students **stood up** when the professor entered the room.
   2 All the photos in the competition were excellent but one **stood out**.
   3 When the millionaire lost all his money, only his true friends **stood by** him.
   4 You should always **stand up for** your beliefs.
   5 When the captain of the team was ill, Freddie **stood in for** him.

2 **Think of your own sentences using:**

   stand up   stand out   stand by   stand up for   stand in for

I'm Mrs Hill. Your maths teacher, Mr Simms, is ill so I'm teaching you today.

Make up a sentence about the picture using *stand*.

7  *Let's look at **turn**!*

1 Can you explain what these phrases mean?
1 When the burger is cooked on one side, **turn** it **over** and continue cooking.
2 Jane invited twenty people to the party but only twelve **turned up**.
3 The ugly caterpillar **turned into** a beautiful butterfly.
4 John was offered a good job at the factory but he **turned** it **down**.
5 The start of the play was a disaster but it all **turned out** well in the end.

2 Think of your own sentences using:

turn over   turn up   turn into   turn down   turn out

Make up a sentence about the picture using *turn*.

---

8  *Let's look at **get**!*

1 Can you explain what these phrases mean?
1 Julie believes that we should **get rid of** zoos and circuses.
2 The police chased the thief but he **got away** in a fast car.
3 Tom is a friendly young man. He **gets on with** everyone.
4 Polly caught a nasty cold but she soon **got over** it.
5 I hate shopping. How can I **get out of** going to the shopping centre?

2 Think of your own sentences using:

get rid of   get away   get on with   get over   get out of

Make up a sentence about the picture using *get*.

---

9 *Let's look at **shut**!*

1 Can you explain what these phrases mean?
1 Your eyelids **shut out** the light when you are sleeping.
2 Business has been so bad that the shop is going to **shut down**.
3 The children are so noisy! They won't **shut up**!
4 The plumber **shut off** the water before he mended the pipe.
5 We **shut** the lost dog **in** the shed until its owner arrived.

2 Think of your own sentences using:

shut out   shut down   shut up   shut off   shut in

Make up a sentence about the picture using *shut*.

Grammar extra | 29

10

Let's look at **go**!

1 Can you explain what these phrases mean?

1 Annette **went on** thinking about Grandma's suggestion.
2 Ben was having such a good holiday. The days **went by** very quickly.
3 Sue **went over** all her work very carefully before the exam.
4 Annie was good at science so she decided to **go into** medicine.
5 I used to like that song but recently I've **gone off** it.

2 Think of your own sentences using:

go on   go by   go over   go into   go off

Make up a sentence about the picture using **went**.

11

make or **do**?

1 Complete the sentences using make or do.

1 Jones was playing in his first match and very quickly _____ his mark.
2 After dinner, Meg and her brother _____ the dishes.
3 I've just tidied the sitting room so please don't _____ a mess.
4 When the waiter brought the wrong pizza, Lisa _____ a terrible fuss.
5 Joe helped his mum _____ the shopping at the supermarket.

2 Write and say. Think of your own sentences with make or do and these words.

a fuss   his/her mark   the dishes   the shopping   a mess

Make up a sentence about the picture using **make**.

12

Let's look at **break**!

1 Can you explain what these phrases mean?

1 Laura **broke off** a rose and put it in her hair.
2 Thieves **broke into** the house and stole valuable jewellery.
3 While we were driving to the coast, the car **broke down**.
4 When do you **break up** for the summer?
5 In 1884, a dangerous disease **broke out** in the town.

2 Think of your own sentences using:

break off   break into   break down   break up   break out

Make up a sentence about the picture using **break**.

Project 1 (Unit 2): What happened next?

Continue the story of *The man at the fountain*. Choose one of these texts.

Philippe followed the man down the main street. After a few hundred metres, he turned down a narrow side street that led down to the dark, wide river. Among the cargo ships, a fishing boat was tied up. The man jumped onto the boat and disappeared inside.

Philippe crept up to the boat and looked in at the window. He could hear voices. The man and three others were gathered round a table looking at a plan of the bank. Philippe was about to turn around and go immediately to the police station when he felt a heavy hand on his shoulder and a rough voice growled, "What are you doing here, boy?"

What happened next? Complete the story.
Use these questions to help you or use your own ideas.

- Who was the man who had hold of Philippe? Was he another member of the gang / a sailor from another boat / a detective in disguise?
- What did the man do? Did he imprison Philippe on the boat? Did Philippe get away? Did he talk to Philippe? What did Philippe say? What did they decide to do?
- Did the thieves get caught? How?

Philippe followed the man down the main street. After a few hundred metres, he went into a smart building with a huge glass entrance and enormous plants inside. Philippe followed him quietly. The man was talking to a woman at the desk. Philippe crept up silently to hear what the man was saying. "… and please tell Joanna I've got the pictures," Philippe heard him say. Suddenly, the man turned round and saw him. "Can I help you?" he asked.

Philippe said, "You were taking pictures of the bank! And your picture is in all the papers!"

The man laughed. "Did you think I was a thief? My picture is in all the papers, it's true, but actually, I'm …"

What happened next? Complete the story.
Use these questions to help you or use your own ideas.

- Who did the man say he was? Was he the owner of the bank / one of the family that once owned the building / a photographer / somebody in films?
- What was his reason for taking the photos? Who is Joanna? Did Philippe meet her? Where? What was the place like? What was Joanna like? What did she say to Philippe?
- Did Philippe stop thinking that the man was the thief? Why? What happened in the end?

Decide what happened. Make notes for your story. Use your notes to write the story. Remember to use paragraphs and direct speech.

Project 2 (Unit 4): A letter to a friend

You have just visited the Adventure Sports Centre. Write a letter about it to your friend.

Paragraph 1: Give a *detailed recount* of *what you did:*
- Who did you go with?
- Did you go on:
  - the aerial runway?
  - the suspended bridge?
  - the vertical slide?
  - the climbing wall?
- Did you try indoor sky diving?
- Is there anything you didn't go on?

How did you feel doing each activity? Excited? Scared? Were you nervous? Did you love every minute? Tell your friend!

Paragraph 2: Say *what you thought* of the Centre:
- **The trainers** were helpful? friendly? annoying?
- **The safety equipment** was too old and dirty? good? new and shiny?
- **The café** was enormous? had great food? was small and crowded?
- **The complex** was near? easy to get to? too far away?

Paragraph 3: Invite *your friend* to come next time:
- **Why** do you want him/her to come with you?
  It's more fun? There are things you can do together? What?
- **When** do you want your friend to come?
  This week? Next week? Next month?
- **How** will you get there? Bus? Car? Whose car?
- **How long** will you be at the centre for?

Ask your friend to tell you if he/she can come.

Do you remember how to set out a letter to a friend? Your address goes here.

> 21 Station Road,
> Newbridge,
> Hampshire
>
> 21st July

The date goes here.

This is how you write a greeting to your friend.

> Dear Harry,
>   I've just been to the Adventure Sports Centre and I wanted to tell you about it straight away. I went on ...

Start your first paragraph on the next line. Indent the first word like this.

Write a short ending.

>   ask your Dad if you can come.
>   Please write back to me as soon as you can.
> From
>   Andy

Finish with 'From' then write your name.

Project 2: A letter to a friend

Project 3 (Unit 5): A great life

Write about someone who you think lived a great life or is living a great life now.

1. **Think about what you already know about the person.**

   What information will you need to find out? How will you find out?
   You can use: books   magazines   the internet

2. **Make notes about the person in three parts.**
   - When and where the person was born, what his or her life was like as a child and young person.
   - The person's life as an adult: what he or she did and what he or she achieved.
   - What happened at the end of the person's life (if he or she is no longer alive) or what the person is doing now.

3. **Write your notes in three paragraphs.**

4. **Write a fourth paragraph. Explain why you think this person had or has a great life. Use these questions to help you or give your own reasons.**

   Do you admire the person? Why?
   Do you think the person achieved special things? What?
   Would you like to be like this person? Why? / Why not?

5. **Write the title: *A great life*. Then write the name of the person. Illustrate your writing.**

Project 4 (Unit 8): What do you think?

Which is more important, the people of the world or wildlife?

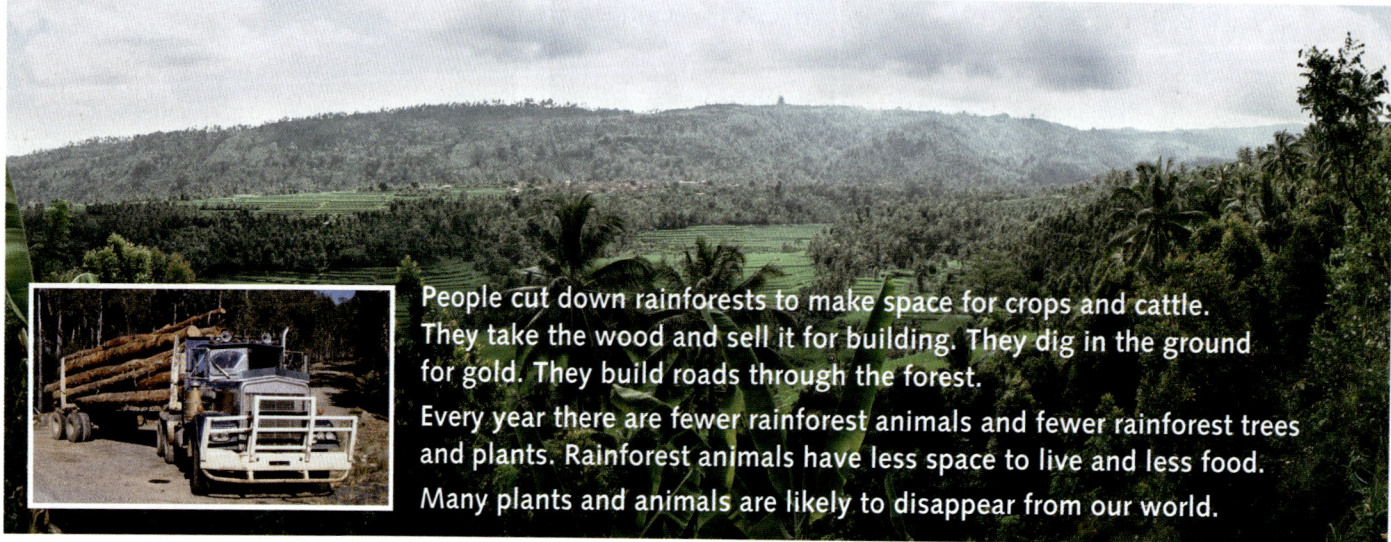

People cut down rainforests to make space for crops and cattle. They take the wood and sell it for building. They dig in the ground for gold. They build roads through the forest.
Every year there are fewer rainforest animals and fewer rainforest trees and plants. Rainforest animals have less space to live and less food.
Many plants and animals are likely to disappear from our world.

What do you think?

Are the animals and plants important?
Does it matter if many of them disappear?

That's terrible. The rainforest plants and animals are important. People should use fewer things so the forests can survive.

Fifty years ago there were 3 billion (3,000,000,000) people in the world. Now there are around 7 billion. In 2050 there will be around 10 billion. They will need more houses, more cars, more oil and more food.
Already, many people do not have enough to eat. They don't have proper houses or cars. Sometimes they don't have enough clothes or any shoes.

What do you think?

Are people more important than wildlife?
Should people take land for what they need?

That's terrible. People need food and homes. They have to use land in order to survive and make their lives better.

Write your views.

Do you agree with Jack?

1. Find out why rainforests are important. Make notes.
2. Write a paragraph. Explain why the trees, plants and animals are important.
3. Write another paragraph. What things could people use less of so the forests can survive? What could you use less of? What can be done for people who don't have enough food?

Do you agree with Holly?

1. Think of all the things that people must have in order to survive. Make notes.
2. Write a paragraph about the things and explain why people need them.
3. Write another paragraph. Explain why it is important for people to survive and live better lives. Should people help wildlife? How?

Project 5 (Unit 9): Amazing eyes in the animal kingdom

In the animal kingdom, eyes have developed in different ways to help animals to survive.

1 Identify the animals in the pictures and match the facts to each one.

1 hammerhead shark   2 hippo   3 frog   4 chameleon   5 eagle   6 owl

a Its eyes are fixed but it can turn its head 270 degrees (or ¾ of a circle).
b It can raise its eyes above the water while its head and body are under the surface.
c It can look at two things in different directions at the same time.
d It can see from side to side, in front and behind but also above and below at the same time.
e It can see underwater very clearly and a special thick lens protects its eyes from sticks and plants in the water.
f It can see a rabbit moving from a distance of 2 kilometres.

2 Find out more about the eyesight of each animal. Think about these questions.
Why does the animal need this eyesight?
Does it help it to find food? How and what food?
Does its eyesight help it to protect itself from other animals?
Is there anything else that is special about each animal's eyes?

3 Make notes about the animals' eyes. Write a paragraph about each animal's eyesight. You can include the facts on this page.

4 Write a title and illustrate your work.

Project 6 (Unit 11): School magazine – group project

Create your own school sports magazine of at least four pages but more if you can. Include: match reports, player profiles, interviews, photos, results, future matches.

Or

Create a school magazine about all activities including sports but also clubs, performances, recitals, news, achievements, special events, etc. Include: reports, reviews, interviews, match results, club meetings, future events, photos.

- Decide how many pages the magazine will be.
- Choose the different articles you want to include.
- Share the work out among the group. Make sure you have a variety of articles – you can't all write match reports or interviews, for example.
- Proofread each other's work.
- Write the work on a computer if you can and print the pages.
- Design a cover and give your magazine a title.

Macmillan Education
4 Crinan Street, London N1 9XW
A division of Springer Nature Limited

Companies and representatives throughout the world

ISBN 978-0-230-03252-1

Text © Liz Hocking, Wendy Wren, Mary Bowen 2012

Design and illustration © Springer Nature Limited 2012

First published 2012

All rights reserved; no part of this publication may be reproduced, stored in a retrieval system, transmitted in any form, or by any means, electronic, mechanical, photocopying, recording, or otherwise, without the prior written permission of the publishers.

Concept design by Anna Stasinska
Page design, layout and art editing by Wild Apple Design Ltd.
Illustrated by Adrian Barclay (Beehive) pp127-130. Kathryn Baker (Sylvie Poggio) pp112. Martin Bustamante (Advocate) pp28, 29, 31, 32, 41, 44, 88, 89t, 90, 94, 95. Grace Chen (Sylvie Poggio) pp8t, 10t, 38t, 71b, 79, 81. Kay Dixey (Graham Cameron) pp98, 99, 100, 102, 104. Peter Dobbin (Pickled Ink) pp18, 19, 20, 22, 25, 58, 59, 60, 62, 64, 65, 131. Anna Hancock (Beehive) pp6, 11, and character heads throughout. Niall Harding (Beehive) pp16, 18, 119, 120, 121, 122, 124, 125. Kate Rochester (Pickled Ink) pp21bl, 61tl+br, 68, 70, 71t + mr, 11r. Mark Ruffle pp42, 61tr.
Cover design by Oliver Design
Cover credit: Alamy/James Ingram (cl), Alamy/Maximillian Weinzierl (tr); Corbis Steve Hix/Somos Images (tl); FLPA/Mark Newman (b); Getty (cr).

The publishers would like to thank the Macmillan teams around the world and Hala Fouad, Hoda Garraya, Caroline Toubia, Samira Mahameh, Adnan Bazbaz, Nisreen Attiya, Mohammed Abu Wafa, Fatima Saleh, Muna Ghazi ,Anna Solovyeva, Tatyana Olshevskaya, Irina Shikyants, Irina Burdun, Elena Mitronova, Inna Daugavet, Olga Pavlenko, Svetlana Potanina, Irina Ostrovskaya, Zhanna Suvorova, Sergey Kozlov, Olga Matsuk, Elena Gordeeva, Marina Kuznetsova.

The authors and publishers would like to thank the following for permission to reproduce their photographs:
Alamy/AEP p36(Tower Bridge), Alamy/Rolf Adlercreutz p126(dentist), Alamy/Allstar Picture Library p47(br), Alamy/John Arnold Images p106(tc), Alamy/Michael Austin p36(swimming), Alamy/Author's Image Ltd p37(Piccadilly Circus), Alamy/Autostock p38(r), Alamy/Yoko Aziz p66(computer game), Alamy/Greg Balfour Evans pp36(Thames cruise boat), 39(l), 86 (terraced housing), Alamy/David Ball p36(London Eye), Alamy/Patrick Batchelder p86(flats), Alamy/Ivan Barta p86(house of glass), Alamy/Blend Images p45, Alamy/Juniors Bildarchiv p66(vet), Alamy/Blickwinkel p79(tl), Alamy/Simo Bogdanovic p16(sketch pad), Alamy/Mike Booth p26(tr), Alamy/Trevor Booth Photography p49(r), Alamy/Kevin Britland p26(cr), Alamy/Buzz Pictures p39(br), Alamy/Catchlight Visual Services pp66(b), 96(br), Alamy/Jacky Chapman p67(tl), Alamy/Richard Cooke p79(cr), Alamy/Ashley Cooper p39(tr), Alamy/David Crausby p66(teacher), Alamy/Cultura Creative p68, Alamy/Cultura pp38(c), 69(cr), Alamy/Robert Estall Photo Agency p36(Tower of London), Alamy/Chad Evans p106(cr), Alamy/Findlay p116(carriage), Alamy/Finnbarr Webster p90(d), Alamy/Finshooting p92(tl), Alamy/Lou Foto p57(tr), Alamy/Joe Fox Motorsport p89(bl), Alamy/Robert Fried p96(pots), Alamy/David J Green/Lifestyle Themes (girl on laptop), Alamy/David Grossman p43(br), Alamy/Thierry Grun p66(photographer), Alamy/Mark Gwilliam p116(airport), Alamy/Robert Harding Picture Library pp17(r), 96(textiles), Alamy/Stephen How pp 109(t), 110, 114, Alamy/hfs001 p36(train), Alamy/Stuart Hickling p16(F1 car), Alamy/Huntstock pp109(r), 112, Alamy/Imagebroker pp 32(tr), 42(tr), 107(r), Alamy/INTERFOTO p49, Alamy/Isifa Image Service s.r.o p49(l), Alamy/Image Source p43(bc), Alamy/James Ingram p89(r), Alamy/Maurice Joseph p76(cr), Alamy/Itanistock p32(bl), Alamy/Justin Kase pp36(cinema), 37(l), 66(tourist guide), Alamy/Stan Kujawa p116(railway station), Alamy/Kuttig/Travel p36(tourists), Alamy/Jim Lane p16(football), Alamy/Lebrecht Music & Arts Photo Library pp52, 55(b), Alamy/Justin Kase p36(cinema), 37(l), 66(tourist guide), Alamy/Richard Levin p117(c), Alamy/Yadid Levy p17(l), Alamy/Pawel Librar Images p117(l),Alamy/LJS Photography pp56(cl), Alamy/Nick Lylak p90(a), Alamy/Manor Photography p96(clothes), Alamy/Mary Evans Picture Library p48(t), p50, Alamy/MBI pp16(family),38(l), 39(tc), Alamy/MI Stock Photos p76(tl), Alamy/Jeff Morgan p37(r), Alamy/Keith Morris pp39(cl), 41, 44(l), 76(tr), Alamy/Nicosan p89(br), Alamy/Oleg p27(t), Alamy/Stuart Pearce p38(tl), Alamy/Photoalto p108, Alamy/Photos 12 p97(r), Alamy/Picture Contact BV p92(r), Alamy/Picture Partners pp39(bc,bl), 44(b), Alamy/Ian Pilbeam p46(c), Alamy/Robert Preston Photography p78(br), Alamy/PSL Images p126(phone), Alamy/Reportage/Archival p47(tc), Alamy/John Robertson p86(Poundbury),

Alamy/Paul Rogers p16(computer), Alamy/Chris Rout p56, Alamy/RT Images p90(b), Alamy/Yulia Saponova p26(br), Alamy/Alex Segre p67(c), Alamy/Ian Shaw p96(cheese), Alamy/Eitan Simanor p86(Cairo mansion), Alamy/Paul Springett p116(traffic), Alamy/Snappdragon p76(tc), Alamy/Doug Steley p56(r), Alamy/Charles Stirling(Travel) p96(fruit), Alamy/Stockshot p38(r), Alamy/Lee Karen Stow p82(t), Alamy/Nik Taylor p92(c), Alamy/Tetra Images p72, Alamy/Travelshots.com pp16(swimming), 36 (street), Alamy/Upper Cut Images p32(br), Alamy/Vario Images GmbH Co KG p107 (br), Alamy/Rob Walls p126(hairdresser), Alamy/Tony Watson p46(r), Alamy/Maximillian Weinzierl pp87(tr), 94, Alamy/Westend61 GmbH p26(tc), Alamy/Travel England/Paul White p8, Alamy/Michael Willis p16(apartment block), Alamy/Woodystock p116(cruise ship); **Art Directors & Trip** p17(t), Art Directors & Trip/Helene Rogers p69(all); **BrandX** p36(Buckingham Palace), 135(owl), 135(hippo); **Bridgeman**/The Stapleton Collection p48(b) Bridgeman/Ken Welsh p54; **Corbis** pp133(tl), 135(frog), Corbis/Bettmann p55(t), Corbis/Deborah Betz Collection p47(l), Corbis/Con Tanasluk/Design Pictures p65(tr), Corbis/Rune Hellestad p47(r), Corbis/Steve Hix/Somos Images p66(fashion designer), Corbis/Ursual Klawitter p56(tl), Corbis/Ocean pp26(tl), 77(green keyboard), Corbis/Stringer/Spain/Reuters p106(tl), Corbis/Paul Souders p29(bl), Corbis/Gustavo Tomsich p5(c); **Creatas** pp28(b), 30; **Digital Vision** p135(chameleon); **FLPA**/Cyril Ruoso/Minden Pictures p78(b), FLPA/Mark Newman p29(cr), FLPA/Ariadne van Zandbergen pp78(bl), 80; **Getty Images** pp16(chess, snakes, exam paper), 27(cl, c), 36(basketball), 39(cr), 75(cl), 40, 78(t), 106(tr), 133(bl&br), 135(shark), Getty Images/AFP p115, Getty Images/AFP p16(tennis), Getty Images/By Pig Flying p106(cl), Getty Images/Andy Crawford p85(all), Getty Images/Tim Graham p126(mall), Getty Images/Wendy Hope p92(cl), Getty Images/Harry How/Staff p107(tr),Getty Images/Martin Ruegner p27(br), Getty Images/Universal Images Group p47, Getty Images/Granitz/WireImage p47(cr); **Goodshoot** p36(Big Ben); **Grapheast** p77(cr); **Image Source** pp43(bl), 89(l); **Kobal**/Lucas Film/20th Century Fox p57(tc), Kobal/Marvel/Sony Pictures p57(l), Kobal/Warner Brothers/DC Comics p57(br), Kobal/New Line/Saul Zaentz/Wing Nut/Pierre Vinet p97(c, l); **Macmillan Australia** pp75(b), 134(c); **Nature Picture Library**/Doc White pp29(tl), 35; **Photoalto** pp75(t), 134(tl); **Photodisc** pp16(house, kitten, insects), p28(t), 82(tr), 84, 135(eagle); **Photolibrary**/Norbert Eisele-Hein p42(tl), Photolibrary/Kim Kirby p36(restaurant sign); **Photostage**/Donald Cooper p117(r); **Rex Features**/20th Century Fox/Everett p57(c); **Science Photo Library**/Gusto Images p87(tr), Science Photo Library/Medical RF.com p87(tc); **Stockbyte** p16(guitar); **Superstock** p134(br) Superstock/Nordic Photos/SuperStock p90.

Commissioned images by **Lisa Payne** pp4, 5, 8(t), 9, 12, 13, 14, 15, 16(tr), 23, 26(tr), 33, 36(tr), 43, 46(tr&br), 53, 56(tr&br), 63, 66(tr), 73, 76(tr), 83, 86(tr), 93, 96(tr), 103, 106(tr), 113, 116(tr), 123, 126(tr), 134(children); **Philip Stills Photography** p46(computer); **Studio 8** pp7, 46(stationary).

These materials may contain links for third party websites. We have no control over, and are not responsible for, the contents of such third party websites. Please use care when accessing them.

Although we have tried to trace and contact copyright holders before publication, in some cases this has not been possible. If contacted we will be pleased to rectify any errors or omissions at the earliest opportunity.

Printed and bound in Spain

2023 2022 2021 2020 2019
22 21 20 19 18 17 16